EARS, EYES, AND HANDS

EARS, EYES, AND HANDS

REFLECTIONS ON LANGUAGE, LITERACY, AND LINGUISTICS

Deborah L. Wolter

Gallaudet University Press   *Washington, DC*

Gallaudet University Press
Washington, DC 20002

http://gupress.gallaudet.edu
© 2018 by Gallaudet University
All rights reserved. Published 2018
Printed in the United States of America

Library of Congress Cataloging-in-Publication Data

Names: Wolter, Deborah L., author.
Title: Ears, eyes, and hands : reflections on language, literacy, and
    linguistics / Deborah L. Wolter.
Description: Washington, DC : Gallaudet University Press, 2018.
Identifiers: LCCN 2018041581| ISBN 9781944838393 (paperback) | ISBN
    9781944838409 (e-book)
 Subjects: LCSH: Literacy--Social aspects--United States. |
    Sociolinguistics--United States. | Students with disabilities--United
    States. | Deaf--United States--Biography. | BISAC: LANGUAGE ARTS &
    DISCIPLINES / Literacy. | BIOGRAPHY & AUTOBIOGRAPHY / Educators.
Classification: LCC LC151 .W655 2018 | DDC 302.2244--dc23
LC record available at https://lccn.loc.gov/2018041581

∞ This paper meets the requirements of ANSI/NISO Z39.48-1992 (Permanence of
Paper).

CONTENTS

FOREWORD

LATE ONE afternoon I landed my two-seat Cessna at a small-town airport in rural Ohio. Upon learning that I was profoundly deaf, the friendly airport manager wanted to know all about FAA-certified deaf pilots who fly under visual flight rules without radio. After our lengthy chat, he invited me on a test flight of a Piper he had just serviced. During the hop, he briefly gave me the controls and nodded approvingly at my skills.

When we returned, a thunderstorm was gathering, and I said, "I'd better overnight here. May I borrow the airport car?" Rural airports often keep such vehicles, mostly old beaters, to allow stranded fliers to find nearby motels.

The manager replied warily, "I don't know. Are deaf people allowed to drive?"

That would have been funny, I am sure Deborah Wolter would agree, if it weren't so appalling. As a profoundly deaf educator, she has suffered similar ignorance and stereotyping from otherwise well-meaning fellow teachers as well as parents despite her impressive academic credentials and more than 20 years of experience working one-on-one with struggling young readers. So have her pupils.

Instead of dismissing such incidents of low expectations, however, she turns them into powerful teachable moments.

In *Ears, Eyes, and Hands*, she explores the deep reasons behind those incidents in stunning, eye-opening detail. These hard knocks have broadened her knowledge and sharpened her responses to inequity and oppression. They have made her an effective advocate for new ways to boost youngsters' lagging skills, elevating them "from learning to read to reading to learn."

This book, however, is not a litany of complaint. In linked essays, Wolter discusses both the richness and frustrations of human communication on the background of her deafness. In some ways this book is a romp on the playing fields of language. In showing us how to steer a course across "our bewildering but delightful world of diversity," she tells stories not only about herself but also about her students, many of the tales as endearing as they are illuminating.

She explores the deeper meanings of the term "literacies." (There are many kinds.) She plumbs the intricacies of reading and the strategies of persuading a pupil to read and to write. She breaks down the process of writing with closely linked detail.

With fierce gusto, she confronts society's stereotyped and shallow ideas about accented English, such as that spoken by African Americans and others whose language and culture lies outside "proper" norms. She wants her fellow educators to avoid easy labels for struggling readers, for they amount to covert segregation of those who are "different." She wants us to open our minds to people with disabilities as well as members of racial and social minorities.

Wolter did so for the children who are her charges, a challenging task because she is deaf and classrooms tend to be noisy. She shows how not only deaf people such as she, but also everyone else, must *learn to listen*—parents, teachers and aides in particular. Listening, she shows, is a surprisingly complex skill. (It is not the same as hearing.) On the way, she demonstrates why speech and language are different phenomena, and why talking about little things is often more important than talking about big things. Most of all, she declares, be kind: "Communication and conversation calls for gentleness and commitment from all parties involved."

She believes schools have become segregated according to misperceived ability, and must adjust and expand their views of what literacy means. Further, they must drain the swamp of dependency on phonics instruction and refill it with more meaningful practices that focus on the message rather than the means and explore the differences between spoken and printed language.

She argues that educators should stop using testing alone to judge the capabilities of readers and rely instead on the rich community of reading: "a village of bookmobiles, ice cream trucks, and recreation supervisors. A village of patient family dogs and doting grandparents. A village of bookstores and friends who wander through them."

At the end of the day, more than a quarter of a century after passage of the Americans with Disabilities Act, we must still clear cobwebs of prejudice from our minds and appreciate diversity for its own sake. We must open our hearts in order to grasp the similarities as well as differences among human beings.

Most of all, we must accept Wolter's powerful argument that making apparently expensive accommodations, such as sign language interpreters and keyboarded communication for the deaf, will help people with disabilities become productive and well-paid members of society who give back economically rather than go on welfare—which can be more expensive in the long run.

Ears, Eyes, and Hands speaks to me in particular. Like its author, I am profoundly deaf. Although we are two decades apart in age, I also grew up privileged in a university town—white, comfortably situated, learning and speaking standard English, and attending progressive schools with complete inclusion in classes and activities. Like her, I grew up to work with words, sounding them out on the twin tympanums of memory and imagination. Like her, I write to be heard. Like her, I strive to *communicate*—and, after reading this illuminating book, I will also try harder to empathize with people and ideas outside my experience, to appreciate other "ways of being."

So, we can hope, will parents, teachers and administrators as well as general readers concerned about the future of American education. This book is for them.

Henry Kisor

Henry Kisor is the author of nine books, including What's That Pig Outdoors?: A Memoir of Deafness *(Hill & Wang/Farrar, Straus & Giroux, 1990) and is co-author of* Traveling with Service Animals: By Air, Road, Rail and Ship Across North America *(University of Illinois Press, 2019).*

PREFACE

deaf

I am deaf.
I am not culturally Deaf. I do not know sign language.
I lipread and speak. I do not hear.
I am not partially-deaf, or hearing-impaired, or hard-of-hearing.
I am not tone-deaf.
I am not deaf and blind.
Nor am I deaf and dumb.
I am just deaf. I have no hearing. I do not hear at all.

EVEN THOUGH I am deaf, language is all around me every moment of my days. I know I do not roll my *R*s or say my *S*s very well. I know better than to ask if I may s(h)it here. I know I say, "Bless you?" in the form of a question, because I'm never sure whether someone sneezed, coughed, or even laughed. I know I still come across new-to-me idioms, quotations, and knock-knock jokes most people learned when they were five or six years old. I know that I substitute more sophisticated words I struggle to pronounce, such as *substantial* and *tenacious,* with first-grade words like *big* and *tight.* I know that my morphology is mixed up and I say that something is *confusely* to me or that it is *cloudying* up outside. I know my grammar is not quite right. I know that I interrupt . . . a lot. I know that I ignore what I don't hear behind me. I know that my voice is either too soft or too loud. I stutter, bumble, stumble, and trip my way through language.

But I also know how to inquire, look up words and phrases, do research, and read. I know that with kindness, humor, and patience all around, I can "hear" and be heard as well.

Many people have supported or contributed to this book. I thank Tamar Charney, Henry Kisor, and Philip Zazove for their insightful suggestions; Jeannie Ballew for her coaching and editorial assistance; Michael Johnson for our courageous conversations; my mother, Dody

Wyman for reminiscing with me; my family and friends for listening to the stories; Ivey Pittle Wallace, who saw my book's strength and carried it to publication; Doug Roemer for his editing expertise, Deirdre Mullervy for shepherding this book through the production process; Donna Thomas for coordinating the production and Valencia Simmons for her marketing assistance; and Angela Leppig for overseeing its publication. I hope that you are graced within these pages to embrace linguistic diversity, create safe spaces, and foster a sense of community, not just for deaf people, but also for people who come from all walks of life.

PART 1

LANGUAGE

INTRODUCTION: DEFINING LANGUAGE

There are no wrong roads to anywhere.
—Norton Juster, *The Phantom Tollbooth*

Language is needed to define language. *Language*, as a single term, has multiple meanings that are used in multiple contexts. Language, by one definition, is the systematic, conventional use of sounds, signs, or symbols for communication and self-expression in a society. Language can be defined as a native or primary language, anywhere from American Sign Language (ASL) to Zulu. Or it can be defined as a type, such as computer language, body language, or animal language. Likewise, speech is the way a person speaks, such as their dialect, or it could be a form of oral communication, such as a graduation speech. The reader who is starting off on the path in this book must keep in mind that there are no wrong roads in language. The ultimate goal is communication and self-expression, but the many paths to get there need adventurous exploration without pretensions and judgment.

WELCOME TO DICTIONOPOLIS!

ONLY ONCE in my teaching career, was I called an unsavory name—
"Dampie—" by a first-grader named Liam. Although the insult is not
a real word, name-calling is one of the lowest forms of argument in a
disagreement. Yet, because I try to listen mindfully and intentionally
without immediately evaluating, judging, or disciplining, I saw this was
clearly not a disagreement. I saw a different perspective, one that was at-
tained by listening thoughtfully. In calling me a dampie, I saw that Liam
was baffled in trying to express a word and trying to get me, as a totally
deaf person, to understand it. In the process of trying to make himself
clear, he was also a bit muddled at the underlying meaning of the word.

Welcome to *Dictionopolis*, a fictional kingdom of linguistic confusion. Language, after all, is a complex, dynamic, and bewildering constellation of world languages and regional dialects—of nouns, adjectives,
verbs, exclamations, conjunctions, prepositions, prefixes, and suffixes;
of jargon, slang, puns, and idioms. Letters and letter combinations have
sounds (phonology), letters combine to form words and parts of words
that have meaning (morphology), words are combined into sentences
following specific rules (syntax), words and phrases have meaning
(semantics), and we use language in context to convey meaning (pragmatics). Language also includes body language, gestures, sign language,
spoken and written discourses, and rhetoric.

During his reading lesson, Liam wanted to remark on additional
things besides black cats, bats, spiders, witches, and ghosts that can come
out of a haunted house than what the book listed. With his pointer finger shaking upward, indicating just one more thing, he said, "dampie."
I thought for a moment, trying to piece together what I was reading
on his lips to the context of the story. "Okay, Liam, look at me and try
again," I said.

Liam looked at me, inches from my face , and said, "Dampie."

I thought for a moment again before saying, "Hmmm, I'm trying to
think of what you mean."

By this point, Liam was a little frustrated. "You know, like YOU are a dampie!"

I sat back, surprised. "I am? Out of a haunted house?"

Liam responded quickly, "NO! But you ARE a dampie!"

By this time, it was very clear to me that he was literally saying *dampie,* but I still had no idea what he meant. So, I came up with a proposal. "Liam, I know you don't like to write, but if you try to put down a few sounds, I might be able to understand what you mean." I handed him a piece of scrap paper and pencil.

Liam wrote: *d . . . m . . . e.* I tried sounding his letters out: "Dam-ee?"

Suddenly, Liam shouted, "Yeah, like this!" Then he stood up and stumbled across my office with arms outstretched and eyes closed. Like a zombie!

With a bonk on my forehead, I exclaimed, "Oh! A ZOMBIE!"

Liam excitedly jumped up and down and cheered, "Yeah!"

But then, with all seriousness, I asked him, "Are you telling me that I'm a zombie too?"

Liam's last words, with his eyes rolling, were "Yeah. It took FOREVER for you to get it."

Here was a clash of language, linguistics, and literacies between the two of us, Liam and me. But we worked through it. Even though Liam was young, English was a second language for him, and I am totally deaf in both ears, relying on both lipreading and the context of the book or conversation. Liam knew what zombies look like and was able to act it out in the end. I don't think he meant to call me a zombie literally, but he didn't have any other way to describe the process of our reaching a common understanding.

Throughout my conversation with Liam, my memory flashed back to a delightful children's fantasy adventure novel I had read as a child. In *The Phantom Tollbooth*, Milo and the watchdog Tock found themselves traveling from Doldrums to the Word Market in Dictionopolis, a kingdom of words, where they sell bagfuls of pronouns, packages of adjectives, an assortment of letters, and even synonym buns. After confusion in the marketplace with Spelling Bee, Humbug, and Officer Short Shrift, both Milo and Tock somehow ended up in a dark prison cell with a Which. I heard my inner voice greet Liam, "Welcome to Dictionopolis!"

Language and conversations about language, like in *The Phantom Tollbooth*, should be approached with humor, warmth, and amusement. After all, smiling and laughing is universal in all languages—mispronounced words or misused phrases can bring about lighthearted chuckles. Unfortunately, this is not always the case. Knowing language itself as a communication system containing grammar and meaning is one thing . . . but deeply entrenched attitudes and stereotypes people hold about language is another can of worms. Although certainly unfair, it is a social phenomenon that people judge a speaker's intelligence, character, and personal worth on the basis of his or her language. However, remaining silent is detrimental to dismantling prejudices and biases within our education systems and society at large. Alas, deaf and hard of hearing people, whether they are part of Deaf culture or are mainstreamed within a multitude of other cultures, carry a narrative of silence.

People with disabilities are generally not thought of as having a political, social, spiritual, or even sexual identity. Instead, they are seen as people to whom something unfortunate has happened. Furthermore, the "science" of studying other people's speech and language, including American Sign Language, especially when it is compared to so-called "standard" English, is so pervasive that it effectively overpowers a different knowledge. Theories, instead, are found inadequate, imbalanced, and sometimes false. If we are serious about addressing inequities in our schools, workplaces, and daily lives, we must do more than just shout about the unfairness we experience. A vague and angry rhetoric will discourage risk-taking among our leaders—politicians, teachers, administrators, parents, and employers—and ultimately maintain the status quo of racism, classism, ethnocentrism, and ableism in our society. But on the other hand, through our passivity, neutrality, or even political correctness in our schools and society, we are unwittingly teaching people that they do not have to tolerate worldviews other than their own. The underlying message is that we do not have to listen to or think about challenging concepts and viewpoints. Thus, children may grow up without learning to embrace, or at least respect, other people's experiences and viewpoints. Some even become judgmental or dogmatic about practices in our daily interactions, labeling them as *right* or *wrong*. It is a fine line to walk between speaking up and potentially facing the disparaging experience of backlash.

* * *

This book is about language, linguistics, and literacies through the lens of my deafness. It is about the inner voices utterly lodged inside my head. My inner voices went largely unheard, because many of my attempts to explain my unique experiences were often and effectively shut down. Some of the common phrases said to me to end my pleas to be heard were "You don't count!" "You're too sensitive!" "You're just playing the deaf card!" "Never mind!" "You're just making this more difficult!" and "Why are you being so dramatic?" Some people will deny that my deafness is even an issue—"I'm in the same boat!" or that deafness is even an advantage—"You're lucky you can't hear!"

Such defense mechanisms were always used by people protecting themselves from my position in standing up—no matter how gently, humorously, or firmly—for myself. Because being deaf is a phenomenon most people cannot fully experience or entirely comprehend, my inner voice is not an angry one, but one of resignation and acceptance. Therefore, my purpose in writing this book is not only to give my voice a place to be heard, but also to serve as a voice for others, particularly our country's most valuable asset—our children. At the same time, I hesitate to offer a voice for others, but instead, to assert, coming from one who is deaf, that we all must *listen*. For all of us are living day to day in a culturally, racially, linguistically, economically, physically, and academically diverse world.

The narratives that follow in this book are my genuine experiences working and interacting with people of all ages from preschool through high school and beyond. Most names and identifying information have been changed to protect the privacy of individuals. Writing about memories and personal history is a particularly unreliable pursuit, because of the haze and healing of time. And we can never be certain of how our life trajectories would have been different had we done things differently. However, I kept notes in journals, on scrap paper and sticky notes, on my computers, and in blog posts. Some memories are indelibly in my mind.

At the end of the day, according to the adage, people won't remember what you said or did; they will remember how you made them feel. And quite often, I felt rejected, devalued, and isolated. Liam, bless his little heart, discovered that acting out a word or a phrase is effective when necessary, and we became quite a captivating team of teaching and learning. Young children often pronounce "deaf" as "death," because of the developmental nature of their speech, but Liam actually got the two words reversed as he was reading about a terrible tiger:

"We're going to hunt for the terrible tiger. We're not afraid of the terrible tiger. We're not afraid of anything." Liam exclaimed, "Wait! EVERYONE is afraid of SOMETHING!"

I leaned back in my chair, readying myself for Liam to unleash a long-winded but usually creative narrative about things to be afraid of, and said, "Oh?"

Liam responded just as he happened to be scratching his ear, "Yeah, everyone is afraid of deaf."

And again, I was perplexed. "Deaf? Like people are afraid of me, because I am deaf?"

Liam quickly jumped up and shouted, "NO! Like this." He demonstrated the act of shooting himself and falling dead.

Welcome to Dictionopolis! In my personal kingdom of words—in a world that does not hear—there is discombobulation, disorientation, and my reflections of language, linguistics, and literacies. Even though this book is divided into areas of communication, this is only for ease of clarity and understanding. All areas involving language, linguistics, and literacy are interrelated and reciprocal. Many people believe that people learn to listen and speak before learning to read and write, but I learned to read before I learned to speak. Some people develop phonemic awareness about letters and their corresponding sounds through learning the alphabet before learning to read. Others learn to read first and then later develop their sense of phonemic awareness. But most people learn both at the same time. Certainly, a solid foundation in oral language helps people to read more easily, but at the same time, reading and writing increases the complexity and nuances of the vocabulary and phrases one learns over a lifetime. Ultimately, readers of this book, most of whom will have normal hearing, will see how to navigate their own lives more mindfully and intentionally in our bewildering but delightful world of diversity through listening, speaking, reading, and writing, and through conversations, literacies, and linguistics.

GO FIGURE

IF YOUNG children are asked how old they are, they most often will raise the number of fingers corresponding with their age and announce proudly, "I'm three!" or "I'm five!" or "I'm ten!" Although it is not usually a good idea to ask a child to guess an adult's age, we know that chronological age doesn't always match with maturity. Most adults prefer to be young at heart, but a few people are so narrow-minded and inflexible that they never seem to grow up. Tabitha, who declared that she was "four!," was asked at our dinner table one Friday evening how old she thought each of us were. Kara, our daughter who was twenty-six, was thought to be ninety-eight years old, while Keane, our son, at twenty-seven, was gauged to be 200 years old. One friend who just recently turned sixty was guessed to be twenty-four. Another friend, at age forty-one, was estimated to be seventeen. And her father was only three years old.

Of course, Tabitha, as a pre-kindergartener, didn't have her ordinals and quantities figured out yet, but it was amusing to the rest of us. At the other end of the age spectrum, Granny, a friend's mother, proudly shared that she was ninety-one while at a clinic, where she had a routine check-up. She didn't have enough fingers to hold up, but she announced her age to anyone within earshot with the same glee as a tyke. Go figure. We all should absolutely be impressed that Granny was leading a long, fulfilling, and healthful life. However, Granny also related that she would be ready to die when she was no longer able to cook a Sunday meal for her large family. It doesn't matter how old we are, we are social animals, creatures of belonging who need companionship.

Although children can be wise beyond their chronological age, adults—even those who are playful—express maturity by being considerate and thoughtful. It is my opinion that a wise responsibility of authors, especially when writing memoirs or creative nonfiction, is to reference their own racial, ethnic, cultural, and linguistic framework. It is not fair to write about other people and other people's children without acknowledging my own view as an author. For example, I own the fact that I am white. I communicate in English. I grew up in a university town rich with diversity and resources. I had parents who took care of and advocated for me. And I always had food on the table and a bed to sleep in.

Furthermore, we must remember that all of us occupy multiple social groups. If we are oppressed (or privileged) in one social group, it doesn't mean that we are always oppressed (or privileged) in other social groups. Tabitha ventured that I was twelve years old, but I was born in 1962 and profoundly deaf in both ears. My birth came just two years after the time when Ruby Bridges, a black kindergartener, needed federal marshals to escort her into a newly integrated school. I was two years old when the Civil Rights Act was enacted to end segregation in public places and ban discrimination based on race, color, religion, sex, or national origin. However, many states continued to exclude from public school children who are deaf, blind, emotionally disturbed, developmentally disabled, or otherwise considered uneducable.

It was not until I was thirteen that the Education for All Handicapped Children Act was passed in 1975. However, long before such laws were passed to protect my educational rights, I was quietly mainstreamed as one of the first children with a disability in my progressive school district. I received early childhood intervention at a laboratory school at Eastern Michigan University (EMU) and was educated in a public school throughout my elementary, junior high, and high school years in Ann Arbor. I was fortunate that my educational opportunities occurred squarely between the years of overt segregation and before the years of covert segregation in special education. If I had been born earlier, I probably would have been placed in an institution with other deaf children. If I were a child much later, I might have been tested several times a year, seen as an underachiever, and placed in a special education resource room with diminished opportunities to strengthen my language and literacy alongside my childhood friends and neighbors. I am lucky to be the age I am.

Literacy development in young children became a fascination of mine during my first days as a playground supervisor. This was way back in 1979, when I was seventeen years old. Interestingly, I had never thought of a career in education. No one in my family was a teacher. My high school counselor at the time simply asked me if I would like an after-school job through their work-study program. I just shrugged my shoulders, nodding, "Sure, why not?" As luck would have it, I was assigned to a preschool in the neighborhood I was living in at the time. I immediately became captivated, and I have worked with young children ever since.

The preschool was a Montessori school situated in a small one-story building nestled among modest single-family homes. There were only two classrooms, a small office, and an equally small kitchen. Because my work-study job was also after "school" for the preschoolers, they were usually outdoors for free play. I was assigned to supervise the playground and make sure the children played safely on the swings, play structures, and with each other. However, on rainy afternoons, we would stay inside and pull out the crayons, markers, and chalk and large pieces of paper. I noticed that many children were not only drawing stick figures, houses, trains, flowers, and the sun, but also scribbling from left to right and even from top to bottom. Some were also writing various letters of the alphabet. I began to see that these letters served as actual words for the children. They were beginning writers! In addition, I would read stories aloud, particularly toward that anxious pick-up time when the number of children dwindled, and the ones who were left were starting to worry if their mom or dad forgot them. After reading to them, I noticed that one or two would take the book from my lap and go off into a corner with it. Observing from a distance, so the children were not aware I was watching, I would lipread them trying to match the memorized lines with their fingers. They were beginning readers!

Without legal protection or accommodations, and without my deafness noted on my application, I was accepted at Eastern Michigan University in 1981, the very university in which I started learning my language and literacy as a three-year-old. Not only did the university have an excellent laboratory school for children with disabilities like myself, but also a highly respected teacher certification program. Even though I had previously taken classes at EMU as a dual-enrolled high school student and was considering taking on a graphic art major, I had no idea about the exceptional standing of their teacher education programs. However, after being promoted from afterschool playground supervisor to assistant teacher at the Montessori school and thoroughly enjoying the role for several months, I made up my mind that I would enter the field of early childhood education. As it turned out, the program at EMU offered both early childhood and elementary teacher certification, which I immediately pursued with conviction and resolve.

Conviction and resolve I surely needed. After one year at college, my primary source of financing was abruptly terminated due to family circumstances. As a result, I matured beyond my eighteen years. For the next three years, while attending class full time, I also worked as much as I could to support myself through college. I still had the job at the Montessori school, so I would rise early in order to open the school at seven every morning, and I would teach until 2:30 in the afternoon. Then, I'd drive back to the campus in my bright orange, rusty, and dilapidated Datsun to make it to my classes at 3:00 or 4:00.

Some of my classes went on late into the evening. There was never enough time to park in the off-campus lot and take the shuttle to the lecture halls, so I parallel-parked on a side street that allowed parking for only two hours at a time. To avoid getting a ticket, I would sneak outside at each class break to rub off the white chalk that the police marked on my rear tire. That way, I thought, no one would know that that my car had been there for more than the allocated hours. This went on for several weeks until a police officer wised up to me, probably recognizing the distinctive vehicle, and slapped a ticket on my windshield one evening. That was the last straw, so I moved out of the dormitories. I became a commuter student while sharing an apartment with my stepsister, who was attending another university nearby. My college years became a tight routine of working, taking classes, doing an intense amount of research, maintaining my notes, and writing papers in order to keep my grades up.

Of course, as anyone gets into the later years of a program, the required courses become more specialized, and some classes are only offered one semester a year. I needed to take an educational methods course co-taught by several lecturers. Unfortunately, one of the lecturers hardly moved her lips when speaking. I couldn't even lipread her on a one-to-one basis. She kept her face down, and all I could see between her parted, thin, and straight brown hair was a small o-shaped mouth and timid, mouse-like eyes. She didn't adhere to the syllabus, and there were no required reading lists. I was utterly lost in that course. Yet at the same time, this lecturer was not at all flexible in making accommodations for me to assure my success. I began to worry that perhaps I wouldn't be able to student-teach and graduate from college. It turned out that my worry was dangerously close to becoming a reality. When I appealed to the department advisor for guidance, we explored several options—taking a different course, doing independent study, or even writing a thesis. However, any alternate option had to be approved by the dean.

The dean and I had never met, but according to my advisor, when the dean found out that I was deaf, she apparently became vehement that there was no way that the university would issue a teaching certificate to someone who doesn't hear. When it was further discovered that I was already well into my third year, the dean decided that I could earn a liberal arts degree but absolutely not a teaching certificate. Apparently, the dean's first and foremost concern was the potential well-being and safety of the children under my watch. Secondly was the importance of the language and literacy development of the children for whom I would be responsible. In her mind, an early childhood environment or elementary school was absolutely no place for someone who was deaf.

When I heard this news, I was quite alarmed and crestfallen at the same time. It being 1984, there weren't any laws granting protections and access to disabled people in college, the workplace, or other public environments. The department advisor was tall, wore conservative attire, and was a formidable presence. Even though she was warm, approachable, and kind, she demanded respect from her colleagues and students. In any event, she was constantly surrounded by students schmoozing her in the auditorium, in the halls, and in her office. She even held various social gatherings at her home. I found myself attending one evening, despite the limited time I had, but I couldn't keep up with the volley of conversations and felt really out of place. Although I didn't desire to vie for her attention, this was a time I *needed* her attention. Yet, I knew that she was walking a tenuous line between my circumstances, being fair to my peers, and the concerns and biases of her superiors.

Although the department advisor and I continued our discussion of what to do about the required course, she warned the dean that a rejection of my teaching certificate could bring a groundbreaking lawsuit. Ultimately, I did not need to withdraw from the class; I was allowed to do independent work within the required framework of the course under the advisor's supervision. In the end, the whole crisis somehow blew over without any civil action, one that I would probably have lost. Looking back, I surmised that my saving grace was years of successful assisting and teaching in early childhood classrooms. It was not like I didn't know what I was getting myself into. No matter, I didn't let my guard down until I finally graduated and had my teaching certificate squarely in my hands. Yet, more than thirty years after receiving my first degree, I am always dismayed to hear about hard of hearing or deaf people who are *still* confronting issues of ableism, because professors, deans, employers, or other people in positions of power view them as incapable of succeeding in the career paths they have chosen. I know of students being denied admission to medical schools, nurses being hired and then immediately fired from their jobs, and student teachers turned away from obtaining teaching certificates.

Although I've experienced my own share of isolation, microaggression, marginalization, and discrimination during my fifty-plus years, I also recognize that I am not alone. Granted, not many people are deaf, but there are personal and societal oppressions, both overt and covert, against racial, ethnic, economic, linguistic, and disability populations as well. A common question asked of me, coming from the framework that I don't hear, is whether I can *think* in words. Of course, I can. I have language just like anyone else. Even though I am deaf and deal with preconceptions and inequity on a daily basis, I am not flawless in my interactions with other populations. But I think about my words and other people's words deeply.

At varying points in this book, the reader may detect prejudice, colorblindness, ignorance, projection, and even defensiveness on my part. These emotional states and reactions exist in all of us. A self-reflective person does not grow older and wiser without revising and refining attitudes, opinions, and worldviews. This book is being published at a specific time, but we all have a lifetime ahead of us for more learning and growing. In my case, I have been, and continue to be, learning how to be hearing and how to be deaf. I'm constantly asking myself: What are the differences? What are the similarities? Do I approach a particular situation from a normal framework, in that everyone is in the same boat? Or do I approach the situation from a disability framework, in that my deafness was the direct cause or issue? Or do I approach the situation from a minority framework, in that my deafness is simply a *diversity* matter? I think and rethink the answers to these questions.

Here's an example of what I mean: I know it is generally rude to interrupt a conversation. So, if I want to interject a comment, I have to decide if I should remain polite, like a *hearing* person, and wait until someone notices me and lets me have a turn to speak. If I see one person is done speaking, I look around to make sure no one else is speaking. But then while I look around, someone else may start speaking; thus, if I speak, I've interrupted that person. In this climate of politeness, it is better not to try to say anything at all. The other option is to let myself be a deaf person and try to partake in the conversation, even if I come across as a bit rude. And in the matter of diversity, there are all kinds of social rules for carrying on conversations. In some cultures, people interrupt each other without causing any hard feelings. In other cultures, the speaker takes offense when someone interrupts. This book encourages readers of all ages to know their own beliefs, values, attitudes, and worldviews while listening to and reading about other people's stories. We should always be open, listen, and see, both inwardly and outwardly.

MAGIC

LANGUAGE IS NOT SOMETHING we often think about. It is something that unconsciously happens during our interactions with others or with print. Yet, when we are confronted with a novel concept about language, it can give us pause. Almost every day, I see people abruptly stop in their tracks to ponder for a moment, when I share that I'm deaf. Some people don't bother to think and scurry off. Some start to ask questions. And others quickly make assumptions about what being deaf means. I not only have to let adults know that I'm deaf and share ways to communicate with me, I need to let children know, too. However, children can come up with some of the most imaginative responses as to how I can communicate:

"Er, um . . . well, er . . . I . . . um . . . I don't know!"—a third-grader

"Vibrations! Right here on the table!"—a fifth-grader

"Sign language! Wait! I'm not signing to you!"—a fourth-grader

"Somehow your brain just picks it up, you know, like aliens or God or something"—a fourth-grader

"Magic"—a third-grader

Language is indeed magical. Even though the process of learning language begins at birth, it is a monumental event for parents and families when their baby says her first recognizable word. Most babies respond to sounds and begin to cry differently for different needs, beginning at birth. By four to six months, their babbling sounds more speech-like, and they can vocalize excitement and displeasure. When they are two or three years old, their vocabulary increases rapidly, and they have a word for almost everything. They can also use two to three words to formulate phrases and ask for things. They begin to listen to and enjoy stories for longer periods of time. By the time they are five years old, they can hear and understand most of what is said at home and in school, and people outside of the family can usually understand their speech as well.

Of course, young children make amusing "mistakes" along the way. They say "*goed*" and "*wabbit*," call all four-legged animals, big and small, "*horsies*," declare that electric outlets are "*pigs*," and make up seemly *wild* and *imaginative* stories. Yet the sheer amount and depth of language-learning in just five short years never ceases to amaze adults watching young children grow. The period from birth to two years old is a critical time for the acquisition of language for all children. However, this period is when deaf and hard of hearing children are deprived of the natural processes that promote healthy language development.

Hearing children born into hearing families do not require special instruction to learn a spoken language. Likewise, deaf children born into Deaf families who use sign language, learn a signed language without special instruction. The greatest risk to deaf children is that they are likely to be born into worlds that do not linguistically accommodate their specific biological characteristics. The latter was the category I was born into—both my parents and all of my grandparents were hearing—but it was magical that I still managed to learn to communicate in spoken English.

I was nearly three years old, "a little terror," when my parents realized I was deaf. At that time, my speech consisted only of guttural sounds. I was becoming very frustrated at not being able to say what I wanted, which resulted in frequent temper tantrums. I was seriously language delayed, not because of my innate cognitive abilities, but simply because I didn't hear or learn the language spoken all around me. Not long after the diagnosis of my hearing loss, my parents enrolled me at Rackham School, a nearby university laboratory school. I was lucky to be there, because it was well before early intervention was the norm and my rights to an education became legal. This was a time when my parents were told that there was nothing they could do about me until I was at least six years old. Then at that age, I would be placed in a separate facility for deaf children or even institutionalized instead of going to school.

The concept of early childhood intervention was not commonplace in the mid-sixties, and the Education for All Handicapped Children Act wasn't enacted until well into the 1970s. Head Start, a federally funded program created to provide comprehensive education, health, nutrition, and parent involvement services to low-income children and their families, was launched in 1965. Eventually, middle-income parents wanted their children to have a "head start" in their schooling as well. Over the years, preschools have become more commonplace, as many children have a single parent or two working parents. We now also hear of competition for elite preschool slots among parents who are willing to pay enormous sums for tuition. Although it may seem that I had a head start on my education, in reality, my opportunity for early intervention was more of a catch-up time before I started formal schooling.

Rackham School, now a beautiful historic building on the campus of EMU, was the first facility in the nation specifically for training teachers in special education. The progressive school opened in 1939 and not only housed the department of special education, but also a school where student teachers learned techniques for educating students with special needs. In addition to classes for "blind and partially-sighted, mentally retarded, and physically handicapped" children, in the terminology used at the time, there were classes for children who were deaf and hard of hearing. And the school contained a speech and hearing clinic, where I went for my therapy sessions. I remember marveling at how everything, from the furniture to the windows, at this school was just my size. Most memorable were the Franklin tiles, known for their handcraftsmanship and rich glazes, decorating the areas around the drinking fountains and along the walls with designs of fish, frogs, crabs, cougars, cranes, and leaves. The school even had a small indoor therapeutic pool, which, in my mind, was a perfect child-sized swimming pool that we enjoyed the use of once a week or so. My years at Rackham were definitely a time when I began to settle down with a sweeter disposition, if not a bit less mischievous, and started to thrive.

At Rackham, my peers and I were taught, quite dogmatically, through *oralism*. Oralism, the use of lipreading and speech, and *manualism*, the use of sign language, have been on opposing sides of a contentious debate that continues to this day, especially with regard to how a child should learn to read and write in English. ASL is far from pantomime or a set of crude gestures; it is well recognized by linguists as a valid language containing phonology, morphology, and syntax. It even contains regional dialects. We did not become a species that is constantly engaged in pantomime with no speech, because of the ambiguity of our gestures. For example, if a person waves his arms up and down, is he talking about a bird itself (as a noun) or a bird flying (as a verb)? Charades can be quite a challenging game for people of all ages. ASL is a real and authentic language akin to other languages, such as English, Russian, and Urdu. There is no ambiguity in signs. Sign languages are specific to the countries in which they originate, and some countries have more than one sign language, just as they have more than one spoken language.

The controversy over which communication method is best for deaf children has been going on since the late eighteenth century. Those who support manualism or sign language believe that the extensive practice of lipreading, listening, and speaking takes too much time away from learning academic content. Additionally, there are some students who do not have enough proficiency with lipreading or speech to participate fully in a classroom or workplace environment. On the other side, people who insist on oralism argue that the use of sign language isolates deaf people further from the wider culture. Ultimately, in suspecting that I had already started lipreading on my own, my parents rejected manualism on the grounds that I would eventually have to learn and function in the hearing world. They worried that if I learned ASL, I would have no one to communicate with in my own family and community.

In elementary school, I remember that many of my friends and classmates asked why I didn't learn ASL, especially when a lot of them were checking out library books on American Sign Language and were trying to learn it among themselves for fun. I always shrugged and tried to avoid a snide response such as, "Then why don't you learn Arabic or Cantonese?" Many of my preschool peers eventually learned ASL as they grew up together. However, in second grade, I moved away from this group to be mainstreamed in my neighborhood school. ASL is not simply a fun medium for deaf and hard of hearing children to communicate with. It is a complex language that is closely tied to a culture and community to which I did not belong.

For decades, linguists, cognitive scientists, and more recently, neuro-scientists have contemplated the question of how children so magically and miraculously listen to, express, and learn language. Children, even those who know sign language as a first language, are not simply sat down and taught how to use language, word by word or sentence by sentence, per se. They are not directly taught how to string together, in grammatical order, a set of nouns and verbs. They are not explicitly taught how to utter consonants and vowels and speak with appropriate pitches and tone. Instead, through interaction with caring adults around them, children—on their own—absorb the vocabulary and rules of language to come up with increasingly complex phrasing, using brand-new combinations of sounds and words or signs to express themselves. Language cannot be a repertoire of responses; the brain must contain a recipe or program that can build an unlimited set of sentences out of a finite list of words. Our vast knowledge of language, whether conscious or not, is wired into our brains. Historically, multiple theories of how children learn language have emerged. One of the first works noting a biological timetable for language acquisition was suggested in 1959 by Penfield and Roberts. By 1967, Lenneberg developed this concept further into the *critical period of language acquisition*. The critical period, as determined by various, but now outdated, studies on feral children, deaf children, second-language learners, and persons with brain damage, pertains to the window of time when the brain is most open to learning language; after this period, learning is much more difficult and less successful. However, almost as soon as the critical period hypothesis was suggested, it began to be, and continues to be, challenged and reconsidered in studies on the plasticity of the brain (for example by Werker and Hensch).

With the alternate term, *sensitive* (or *optimal*) *period*, Werker and Hensch continued to reflect on the fact that windows do not always open and shut abruptly and may even never close completely. Language acquisition is characterized by multiple critical and sensitive periods, with different onsets and offsets and different dynamics. For example, the acquisition of syntax and speech perception has openings and closures at different points in development, but vocabulary acquisition remains open across the life span. In my case, my brain managed to be open enough to learn language as late as I did.

The topic of a critical period for language acquisition remains controversial and presents a continuing research challenge in developmental neuropsychology and neurolinguistics. However, we would certainly never tell families and schools not to waste their time nurturing language, simply because children are born with a biological instinct for language. Our brain's biological equipment and the language our society uses around us are both indispensable in acquiring language. It is absolutely true that nature and nurture play a large role in children's language development.

But what happens when children cannot hear the language swirling around them? Children who are born with a hearing loss or whose hearing loss occurred before they began to speak are prelingually deaf. These children have the biological capacity to learn language, but because nearly 96 percent of them have hearing parents, they have limited, if any, access to spoken or signed language. As a prelingually deaf preschooler, I had to physically learn how to speak. I knew how to read the word *cat* very early on, but I had to learn that the word was made up of sounds I could not hear: c-a-t. A speech therapist taught me how to make each sound and then blend them together to form the word. I received instructions on where to place the back, front, and sides of my tongue in my mouth, how to make the air flow, how to use my voice, and how to pull it all together to form spoken words. Even today, my speech is not perfect; but, for the most part, it is intelligible.

Researchers say that when babies babble, they produce all the possible sounds of all human languages and can randomly generate phonemes from Japanese to English to Swahili. As children learn the language of their parents, they narrow their sound repertoire to fit the model to which they are exposed. Children all over the world learn more than one language without developing speech or language problems. Most children, even those who are deaf or hard of hearing, have the capacity and facility to learn more than one language. There are many advantages to being bilingual or multilingual, such as being able to learn new words easily, being able to use information in new ways, having good listening or observation skills, and being able to communicate with people from other countries. Even though hearing is crucial to attaining the ability to speak, many deaf and hard of hearing people, including myself, develop intelligible speech. However, keep in mind that speech is the oral expression of language. Language can certainly be acquired and expressed visually through sign language, lipreading, and print. Furthermore, just as hearing people all over the world can learn more than one language, deaf and hard of hearing people can be multilingual, either with a written/spoken language and a signed language, or with several signed languages.

In fact, although the debate between oralism and manualism continues somewhat today, the National Association of the Deaf currently supports bilingualism in educational settings. The association points out, in a positive manner, that children can be fluent in both ASL and in English. They are now asserting that literacy development should begin at an early age, and schools should be held accountable for ensuring that deaf children reach age-appropriate milestones in reading and writing English.

Even though I didn't learn ASL, I understand why people use it. I just didn't grow up with it as part of my culture. As an adult, I could learn ASL if I wanted to, just as the next person who might want to learn conversational Spanish or German. I do, however, believe that it is crucial for young children to have a first language, no matter if that language is spoken or signed. And the rest of us, like my students who thought I can communicate through vibrations, like aliens or God, or via magic, should be open-minded enough to seeing how language as a phenomenon—accents, dialects, and all—is embodied in our cultures, society, and ways of being.

PART 2

LISTENING

INTRODUCTION: DEFINING LISTENING

No one is as deaf as the man who will not listen.

— PROVERB

LISTENING IS THE ABILITY to attend to environmental sounds. It is also the act of comprehending language. Too often, listening is considered strictly in auditory terms, that a person must hear in order to listen. It takes much more than just hearing to listen intentionally, mindfully, and thoughtfully. Listening from both the head and the heart is a cognitive process of receiving information, grasping messages, feeling emotions, and responding to needs. Deaf and hard of hearing people have a heightened sense of auditory awareness, an awareness that people with normal hearing acuity may easily take for granted. They know full well that there are sounds to indicate dogs barking, elevator bells dinging, or trucks rumbling by. They know full well that people use sounds to communicate with each other. However, there are many forms of listening—using residual hearing, acknowledging visual and tactile cues that indicate the presence of sound, lipreading mouth movements, using gestures and body language, reading captions, and watching sign language. Communication is all around us. But people can turn a deaf ear, even if they can hear. How well we "listen" inherently depends on the depth and breadth of our willingness to pay attention.

THE LITTLE TERRORS

CALEB, A LIVELY young first-grader with normal hearing whom I had just met, and I, with deafness, came up against people who did not first consider our inability to *hear* but quickly assumed that we were simply not listening. Caleb was brought into a small conference room, where I was finishing up paperwork after a long and tiring meeting, seemingly in trouble for not listening to his teacher. He was sat down on a chair, too tall for his feet to reach the floor, and his face was barely visible across the boardroom table from me. His teacher placed a blank sheet of paper and a pencil in front of him and told him to copy the words she wrote on the whiteboard:

Dear Mrs. Snyder,

I am sorry for not listening.

Caleb.

When he was done, he would be permitted to return to his classroom, presumably with better behavior for listening. The moment Mrs. Snyder closed the door, leaving us both with paperwork to complete, Caleb slid down from his chair to explore every nook and cranny of the conference room. There was an unstated assumption that I would supervise him, but without knowing what had happened, I avoided initiating a discussion with Caleb and expected that he would follow through with his teacher's request on his own. Therefore, left to his devices while I feigned working at my laptop computer, Caleb crawled under the table and found an assortment of pens and pencils, paperclips, a laptop computer charger, an empty water bottle, and dropped tissues. He brought them up one by one and set the items on the table in front of me. Then he went over to the four-drawer filing cabinet in the corner and pulled out the tabs labeling the contents of each drawer from their metal slots. He placed the four tabs in a neat row next to the things he found from under the table.

Caleb wandered over to the large windows and peered outside for a moment until his attention was diverted to a dead long-legged spider on the sill. He carefully picked up the spider by one of its legs and added it to the collection of items on the table. Finally, Caleb, going around the boardroom table and spotting the telephone, announced to me, or perhaps just to himself, that he was going to try to call his daddy. At that point, I reminded Caleb that he was there to copy the note to take back to his classroom. I gently steered him back to the chair where his paper and pencil were waiting. I reread the note on the whiteboard for him, pointing to each word. He looked up at me with wide eyes and emphatically stated that he was *not* sorry. The classroom was so noisy that he had no idea what he was supposed to listen to. In fact, he said that he was just minding his own business when he found himself taken to the office. And now he wanted to call his daddy.

There I was, not knowing exactly what brought Caleb to the office in the first place, finding myself in a spot. Mrs. Snyder was long gone. So, I negotiated with Caleb, explaining that his (and my too) ticket out of the conference room was to write a note. To my great relief, Caleb agreed to write:

Dear Mrs. Snyder,

I will try to listen better.

Caleb.

When he finished, I watched him proudly strut back to his classroom, note in both hands. The next morning, Mrs. Snyder thanked me for watching Caleb while he was writing his note in the conference room. I told her that Caleb said he wasn't sorry and wasn't sure what he was supposed to listen to. I wondered out loud if maybe he had trouble hearing or understanding something. Mrs. Snyder insisted that Caleb's hearing was perfectly fine, and she went on to explain that he was just a "little terror." She also added that she wanted to begin the referral process for special education, suspecting that Caleb may have an attention deficit disorder, oppositional defiant disorder, or learning disabilities, because he seemed to constantly move about in the classroom ignoring everything.

Effective teaching is a tricky proposition, requiring one to walk a fine line between objectivity and compassion. Even so, teachers, being human and working with a wily group of young children after all, carry their own level of tolerances, emotional baggage, and entrenched memories of how school should be run. Mrs. Snyder lost her patience with Caleb the morning she brought him to the conference room. She used a commonplace but outdated and ineffective method of school discipline. And she carried a deficit mind-set that something was wrong with Caleb, something beyond her teaching capabilities and necessitating special education. At the same time, I had to push aside my reaction to her treatment of Caleb, triggered by my own memories and emotions. And I had to hold my judgment, because I had no information on what exactly happened between Caleb and Mrs. Snyder that morning. Yet, knowing full well what it is like to not hear and not always knowing what I am supposed to listen to, I found myself feeling a tad bit defensive for Caleb. After all, even children as young as Caleb deserve a voice too. Perhaps he *really* didn't hear or know what he was supposed to listen to. I couldn't help but feel connected to Caleb for I, too, was described as quite the "little terror" when I was young.

My parents did not fully realize I was deaf until I was nearly three years old. Apparently, it's a small wonder that I even survived long enough for them to find out. Until my baby brother came along, my parents—barely beyond their teenage years in the early sixties—never knew that toddlers are not usually like the monster that I was. My mother had attended just one year at a prestigious eastern university, where her parents and previous generations of her family had endowed, enrolled, taught, administrated, or were otherwise part of the collegiate life there. My father, just a year older, was a student there too. Despite their age, they married and soon found their way to the university in Ann Arbor, where I eventually grew up. Marrying young was the norm at that time, as was the cultural expectation that mothers would be homemakers and fathers would be breadwinners. The two-bedroom townhouse my parents lived in wasn't large, but it had sunny windows, wood floors, coved

ceilings, and a small basement. Situated in a historic neighborhood surrounded by large rolling green spaces in a park-like setting, it was a perfect place for starting a family. Little did they know that this idyllic hope
for their future family and home life was going to be challenging.

I was a quiet baby when my parents first brought me home from
the university hospital, crying only briefly when I was hungry. My only
known defect at the time was a small bruise on one side of my face,
which now remains as a faint dimple. Within a matter of months, I
grew robustly from rolling over to crawling to walking to climbing in
rapid succession. I began to require constant watch, literally twenty-four
hours around the clock. My parents' biggest issue was to somehow get
some sleep and know that I, and the household, would be safe. I was
always climbing out of my crib to go off and explore. I got into just about
everything in the house, including playing in the dirt of my mother's
houseplants, finding the bananas on top of the refrigerator, and dragging my little rocking chair to the sink to wash all of the silverware and
dishes from our drawers and cabinets.

Although my sleep-deprived parents devised many ways to keep me
in my crib at night, I found many creative ways to get out of it. One such
strategy involved my mother taking a baby blanket and sewing button-
holes every few inches around the perimeter, finding some rope, and lac-
ing this blanket to the rim of my crib rails, thus creating a nifty cover to
keep me in. Apparently, this strategy caused me considerable distress,
leaving me screaming for a long period of time. When suddenly all was
quiet, my nervous parents came in to check on me. To their exasperation,
they found me asleep on top of the blanket, using it as a comfortable ham-
mock. Finally, my father resorted to reversing the lock on my bedroom
door. Alas, their problems didn't stop there. One day, after my mother
injured her back, I somehow locked my father in my bedroom. Realizing
what I had done, I was in fits of giggles, very pleased with myself that I
had contained both my parents. My mother couldn't get up, and I refused
to let my father out. As innocent as I was, this began a supposed game
of maintaining my power over my parents. They had no idea I was deaf.

Their final straw with me occurred after my jaunt into the kitchen
while they were asleep. I, only two and a half years old, ventured to cook

by mixing flour and eggs, crushed shells, and all into a pot. I put the pot on the stove, and yes, turned on the stove. Then I took all the silverware from a drawer and placed them into an empty Saltine cracker box, which back then was made of tin. I bumped the box while "cooking." The crashing sound of all the silverware onto the floor woke my parents up. My parents, weary and exhausted, were once again outdone by their mischievous offspring—the one who wouldn't listen.

These were the stories told to me time and time again. Every time I heard a version or two of them, my exasperated inner voice kept asking, "If I couldn't hear or speak, wouldn't you think I had to *do* something about it?" If I wanted some bananas and didn't know to how ask for them, then surely I would climb up to the top of the refrigerator and help myself. It made no sense to me why I couldn't play with silverware, wash dishes, or cook in the kitchen in the middle of the night. Only when my parents found out about my deafness, learned to get my attention, taught me how to listen, and made sure I understood them did my behavior improve considerably and my disposition sweeten.

The adults around Caleb and me assumed that we were simply not listening. It did not occur to them that we just didn't hear. Caleb was in a noisy classroom, minding his own business, and I am indeed deaf. Caleb's teacher quickly rejected the idea that he may have not heard what he was supposed to hear. It even took some time before my parents and grandparents on both sides of my family began to question my hearing acuity. They saw that I responded somewhat to their attempts to talk to me. Out of sheer necessity, I must have been quite an early lipreader. When some members of my family tried banging pots and pans loudly behind my back, somehow I turned around to see. They did not know the extent to which deaf and hard of hearing people can sense vibrations from loud noises or maintain a wide peripheral vision to monitor their surroundings. But as I grew, they noticed that my speech contained very guttural sounds, and I was becoming increasingly frustrated at not being able to make clear what I wanted or needed. It was then that I started to be heard. And when I gently supported Mrs. Snyder's idea of hearing and listening, Caleb started to be heard as well. Instead of quickly assuming that Caleb had attention deficit disorder, oppositional defiant disorder, or learning disabilities, she began to pay more attention to the noise level of her classroom. Caleb was not the only one who benefited from her awareness; all of his classmates did as well.

The importance of listening well is paramount for everyone of all ages, regardless of hearing acuities. Listening is an ability that has a positive impact on language acquisition and literacy development, behavior management, social skills, and academic and workplace successes. It is unfortunate that hearing and listening is a sense most people too often take for granted. According to sources sought by Harrington, Helen Keller, a deaf-blind woman known for her leadership in suffragist and pacifist movements, in noting the differences between deafness and blindness, wrote,

> The problems of deafness are deeper and more complex, if not more important, than those of blindness. Deafness is a much worse misfortune. For it means the loss of the most vital stimulus—the sound of the voice that brings language, sets thoughts astir and keeps us in the intellectual company of man.

A common phrase, noted by Harrington, attributed to Helen Keller is that blindness cuts us off from things, but deafness cuts us off from people. Much listening, even among people who can hear, is passive, unquestioned, and superficial. Poor listening leads not only to incomplete internalization of ideas, but also to misunderstanding. Listening is probably the least understood of the four modalities of communication (listening, speaking, reading, writing). Because listening seems developmentally and intrinsically instinctive and automatic, it makes sense that most people put very little thought into hearing, listening, language, and even cognition—at least until something goes wrong.

Both Caleb and I started our young lives being characterized as little terrors, because, in the words of adults around us, we were not good listeners. However, distinguishing between hearing and listening is important. *Hearing* is a physiological phenomenon; *listening* is a psychological act. It is possible to describe the physical process of hearing through acoustics and through the mechanisms of the ear, but describing listening as a cognitive process (attending, comprehending, and responding to sound or speech) is much more complex.

Listening is the process of receiving, constructing meaning from, and responding to spoken and/or nonverbal messages. One doesn't always need to hear in order to listen. Oliver Sacks, a neurologist and author, remarked that "deafness as such is not the affliction; affliction enters with the breakdown of communication and language." Certainly, the assertion by I. King Jordan, the first deaf president of Gallaudet University, that "[d]eaf people can do anything except hear" should also apply to their listening skills. Although I am deaf in both ears, if given the opportunity to lipread or read print, I am perfectly capable of listening to and grasping messages being conveyed. Even little terrors, like Caleb and myself when I was young, can and do learn to listen. At the same time, all of us, regardless of our hearing acuity, must learn to listen and to listen well. Then, and only then, can we come to the point where we can listen to our little terrors just as well.

ONE BALL OF CONFUSION

SOME PEOPLE take delight in being around children. Because young children easily befriend people just their size, an adult who gets down to the children's height—all the way down onto the floor to interact with them at their eye level—effectively becomes a kid magnet. Gentle rough housing, laughter, and delighted squeals may ensue. Other people, however, find children downright scary, especially when they are having meltdowns. Yet, it is just a matter of understanding where children are coming from, because for them, and the adults around them, life can be one big ball of confusion.

Like Caleb in the last chapter, Jake found himself exiled from the classroom and planted on a chair just outside the principal's office. Jake was a second-grader, and his toes barely touched the floor. A stuffed rabbit, presumably belonging to the last child who sat in that chair, was splayed next to his feet, but he had not noticed it. Bewildered as to how he got there, Jake cried furiously for more than several minutes, making the school secretary decide it was time for her to take a bathroom break. She looked at me, realized my deafness might be an advantage, and pleaded with me to stick around until she got back.

I sat in a chair near Jake and noticed the pile of children's books on the side table sandwiched between us. I picked up one and began to read. Silently, just to myself. When I was done, I picked up another one, paying no attention to Jake. I learned long ago that a good rule of thumb in dealing with meltdowns is to never engage with the child until he or she is able to hear a whispered voice. I wasn't ignoring Jake, but just by being near him, calmly reading, must have provided some comfort . . . or at least, some interest. It was not long before Jake began to settle down. Continually wiping his nose with his sleeve, Jake picked up a book. He flipped through a few pages and put it back on the table. He looked at me, sniffling, with questioning eyes, asking if he could look through some more. I nodded and handed him a few to browse. By the time the secretary returned, Jake was slouched down on the seat, with his knees and feet hanging over the armrest, fully engrossed in a graphic novel about Captain Underpants.

I had no idea what landed Jake in the main office that day to wait for the principal. However, I knew from various team meetings with teachers and the principal that Jake was in trouble a lot, not only with his behavior, but also apparently with his reading in his classroom. This became the chicken-and-egg dilemma. Was his behavior a result of struggling to learn to read, or was he struggling with reading because of his behavior? But here he was, curled up and reading a book that was well above his grade level. And I could lipread that he was reading out loud to himself, not just looking at the illustrations and flipping pages. I started to wonder if Jake was actually having difficulty with his hearing or listening in his classroom. I brought my concern to the secretary, who was much relieved that Jake had quieted down, and we pulled out his file. In going through the various documents, we discovered that chronic allergies and frequent ear infections were noted on Jake's physical and vaccination forms. Jake's world of sound was likely muffled.

Elementary school classrooms, as quiet places of study, exist only in a perfect world. Many elementary schools across the nation, including Jake's, require a 90- to 120-minute block of uninterrupted time for literacy instruction and practice. A literacy block can include listening to an adult reading aloud; exploring letters, sounds, and words; reading or writing independently; and reading and writing with peers. The most important features of a literacy block are guided reading lessons and a writers' workshop in which teachers work with small groups of three to six children, who have similar instructional needs. Although the teacher is working with one group, usually at a small horseshoe table, other groups of children are rotating at "centers." This allows children to practice their skills as authentic and purposeful readers and authors. Such centers may contain a spot for listening to books on electronic tablets, a mini library complete with pillows and beanbag chairs for reading independently, a large board for practicing phonics using magnetic letters, or a table for writing about a book they read or for writing in a journal.

The classroom may have a cozy corner for community volunteers to read aloud to some children and a side table complete with blank paper, a stapler, and all kinds of markers, crayons, and pencils for making books. For younger children, there might be a play area, say a restaurant complete with recipes, grocery lists, menus, waiter/waitress pads, and receipts. For older children, there may be a place to work on a project, such as a science report, a persuasive piece for social studies, or a letter to a local veteran. In the midst of all this busyness, there might be several adults—interns, special education teachers, therapists, aides, parents, and community volunteers—to support children in their literacy development.

In a literacy block that is functioning smoothly, children know exactly which center they are to visit each day. They usually follow a large chart displaying the symbols for each center, days of the week, their names, and their assigned groups, and the teacher might use a bell to signal a rotation. Most centers, like the listening center or the mini library, are routine and familiar to the children, but clear directions are given ahead of time for the centers that have new or changed activities. The noise level is usually deliberate and even pleasant when all of the children are fully engaged in their language and literacy learning and practice.

Although this block of time can be rich in language and literacy and delightfully open-ended for exploration, it can potentially be quite confusing and noisy. Not all literacy blocks are organized well, and in an unpredictable world of young children, there is high potential for things to go wrong. Some teachers allow children to randomly visit the centers of their choice. Some children break the rules of their groups or centers. Some centers are designed well above or far below a child's ability or interest level. Some centers might be missing materials, such as paper, pencils, markers, or a set of magnetic letters, needed to complete the activities. And other centers are visited by a larger group than the space can accommodate. Even though I don't hear the hubbub, making my way around in classrooms during literacy blocks can be particularly challenging.

Because the principal was not available to discipline Jake that day, it was left up to me to see what I could do to help him go back to his classroom, a task I always dread. I didn't bother asking what happened, for Jake himself probably didn't know. Furthermore, although it is normally difficult for hearing people to comprehend young children, as they try to formulate their thoughts and words and articulate their side of the story in a coherent manner, it is much harder for someone who is deaf. By nature, young children love to talk, but I'm not always sure what they are saying. Admittedly, having some background on the topic that a child is talking about helps me immensely. For example, if a child misses school because of a family trip, and I have no idea where they went, it is more challenging to figure it out. Most of the time, it takes me longer than hearing adults to catch on. Sometimes it only takes another nearby adult to mention just a few key words of what the child is talking about, especially if we are in bustling hallways or out on the playground. However, even if I'm not understanding everything, young children will continue to talk and talk and talk. This even happens to adults who can hear just fine; they completely tune out their little chatterers.

I get to know each child on my caseload individually, so my interactions with him or her eventually come easily, especially when I get down to the floor to lipread them at their eye level. But I didn't know Jake well. I didn't know his teacher well. And both of them didn't know me well either. I didn't know what happened that got him sent to the main office. And I needed take him back to his classroom.

Jake and I stood just inside the classroom door holding hands, knowing we were stepping into unknown territory. Neither of us knew what to do next. The teacher was busy with a guided reading group. A small sign, posted on a pencil stuck into a wad of putty, reminded the children not to interrupt. I looked all around the walls for a chart that would explain which center Jake was to visit and found none. So, I asked Jake, still holding my hand, what was his favorite center was. He pointed to the listening table, where there was a set of tablets and earphones, but we could see it was already full of children. So, Jake decided to visit the writing table, where he could draw pictures and talking bubbles for his characters, like in *Captain Underpants*. I noticed he was still holding that book in his other hand and told him that it was a good idea. I thought it most important for Jake to be motivated and fully engaged in reading and writing during his literacy block, so we made our way toward the writing center with Captain Underpants in mind.

Because I can't hear anything in noisy classrooms, it is quite difficult for me speak and to be heard or understood by others in that environment. I am unable to adjust the level of my volume as needed to compensate for the ever-changing ambient and excessive noise levels. Most of the time, I'm barely heard by one child, and other times, especially during a sudden lull, the entire class hears me. Furthermore, when I am observing or supporting a child, I'm not always sure of what's expected of me. But the quandary is that I often struggle with being heard in my very attempt to ask what the expectations are! More than once, I've been chided for being in the wrong place or for teaching the wrong concept. And the chiding always comes from an adult—never a child—for young children's minds are clean slates. Children do not have a lifetime of learning restraint and judgment behind them. At least, not yet. They do not worry about what is socially or politically correct, so there is no tension or awkwardness. They are naturally curious and egoistical. They honestly don't care about how quiet or loud I am. If they want attention from me, it doesn't matter to them how they get it. If I don't hear them, they will often physically sidle up to me and tap my shoulder, pull my arm or leg, or even turn my face to look at them. So, one can see how Jake and other young children and I can get along imperfectly but just fine!

Adults, on the other hand, are way scarier to me than children. As it turned out, I didn't take Jake to the correct center that day. Not only that, Jake was rebuked for making comic books instead of working on the assignment given earlier in the morning, and I was reproached for encouraging him to read comic books. Apparently, we had "ignored" the teacher's call behind us when we were wending our way to the writing center. We did not hear her. It is not uncommon for me to look up and suddenly realize that I misunderstood or didn't hear something, because scorns, frowns, and eye rolling are shot my way with exasperation or disapproval. My credibility as a literacy consultant gets questioned, and I am left feeling humiliated. My inner voice quickly has to remind myself that I am not a child but simply deaf. Sometimes I have a chance to explain the ramifications of deafness, and other times, I don't. Jake, however, was powerless as a child and not only that, this was the second time he was in trouble that morning. Even though I am an adult and know full well how deafness can unwittingly land me in precarious situations, I can still identify with Jake's feelings of bewilderment and shame in his classroom.

Too often, the adults around Jake and me assume that because most everyone else is doing fine in a literacy block, we should be too. But Jake wasn't hearing too well at the time, and I am deaf. We are both easily confused and stressed in busy and noisy environments. And because we were not behaving "normally," the teacher assumed we were not listening or cooperating. We were seen as having a deficit in our minds or capabilities rather than as persons who simply did not hear something or other. Just like Caleb, Jake was also thought in educational team meetings to have an attention deficit disorder, oppositional defiant disorder, or learning disabilities. Back when I was a child, these disorders were not commonly known, but if they had been, I would probably have received the same diagnoses.

Diagnoses and treatments of attention deficit disorder, oppositional defiant disorder, and learning disabilities have been controversial among pediatricians, educational psychologists, school social workers, teachers, and parents for years, especially in light of the highly demanding curriculum in our public schools and in regard to the use of prescribed stimulants and their side effects. However, Jake and other children who don't hear very well are indeed inattentive and squirmy, particularly in unstructured and noisy classrooms having highly verbal teachers. They can appear defiant when they are not able to hear or understand parental or teacher requests. And they certainly don't learn very well without supports and accommodations. Furthermore, because many young children, like Jake, are prone to colds and ear infections, it's safe to assume that some are really not able to hear well at times. Because my role only involved literacy, I pointed out to the educational team that Jake was reading *Captain Underpants* and wanted to write his own comic story. I reminded them that hearing (and vision) should be ruled out first before assuming any other conditions. In the end, Jake's mother took him to his pediatrician and found that indeed, his ears were plugged up from allergies and ear infections. Jake's behavior improved significantly as a result of both medical care and better awareness from his teacher.

On the other hand, even if a child's hearing acuity is found to be within the normal range, we should be aware of the impact of inferior acoustics in schools, particularly those housed in old buildings. After all, Caleb, who had normal hearing, complained about the noise in his classroom. He had no idea what he was supposed to listen to before finding himself taken to the conference room to write a note of apology. Jake didn't mention anything about noise in his classroom but was equally perplexed at being sent to the school office.

According to the Acoustical Society of America, many educators feel it is important to improve acoustics in classrooms used by children like Jake, who have trouble hearing, but unnecessary to do so in those used by children like Caleb with normal hearing. Many populations of children with "normal hearing" also benefit from better classroom acoustics, including children with learning disabilities, those with auditory processing issues, and those for whom English is a second language. Another group for whom learning is especially dependent on good acoustics are young children who are unable to "predict from context." Excessive noise and reverberation can interfere with speech intelligibility by as much as 75 percent, resulting in reduced understanding and therefore reduced learning. In fact, many studies reveal that classrooms with greater external noise are more likely to have lower student achievement. Therefore, all environments benefit from placing some rugs or carpets in the room, placing soft tips on the bottoms of chairs and tables, hanging window treatments such as curtains or blinds, hanging soft material such as felt or corkboard on the walls, placing tables at an angle around the room to interfere with the pathways of sound, and turning off noisy equipment.

Most of us are well aware that we raise our voices in response to an increase in background noise. This is called the Lombard effect. The Lombard effect, the adjustment of vocal intensity, happens involuntarily when background noise levels change. Even though the phenomenon is not truly a physiological reflex, simply instructing children to keep their voice levels down does little to inhibit it. Poor classroom acoustics can also affect teachers. Teachers are more likely to have voice problems, because of the strain on their voices from talking loudly to overcome poor classroom acoustics for most of their workday. Creating more organized and quieter environments benefits all of us.

On the other hand, we all know that children—and even adults— are known for tuning out. Adults are familiar with children who seem to doze off, daydream, wander around, or otherwise appear to stop listening. Both Jake and Caleb were described as children who seemed to constantly move about and ignore everything. There are numerous studies that highlight the typical "teacher-talk-dominated" classroom experiences of many children—one study, by Rowe, of which eloquently referred to as "the sea of blah." Too often, children suffer through long-winded explanations, even if such explanations are reasoned and well-intentioned. Teachers are prone to repeating directions, to offering constant reminders, and to using voice-overs in announcing and informing all kinds of activities. Children need adults around them to speak with brevity; they actually understand more when adults speak less. A skillful use of silence and wait time is powerful, for it provides time for children to think, rehearse what to say or do, and respond.

Listening is a complex process for both people with normal hearing and people having hearing losses. Jake and Caleb were accused of not listening. However, there is a distinction between being alerted (hearing), active listening, and obeying. Too often, people roll all three concepts of listening into one big ball of confusion. Perhaps Caleb and Jake really didn't hear. Perhaps they were distracted by something in the room. Perhaps they were not listening carefully. Or perhaps they were indeed listening but chose to disobey. Therefore, it is helpful to recognize five dimensions of listening competency: *cognitively* (understanding how complex the listening process is), *affectively* (being aware of emotional barriers one experiences in listening), *behaviorally* (fully focusing on the speaker), *contextually* (being aware of the settings and using different skills to better listen in them), and *ethically* (avoiding immediate judgment about messages by listening to arguments and evaluating them). Mindfully thinking about the complex listening processes and creating quieter environments for *all* children and adults, including Jake, Caleb, and myself, is an important first step to increase opportunities for hearing, listening, and learning.

SECOND-GRADE OTOLARYNGOLOGIST

ALTHOUGH I AM able to lipread and speak—and function in my everyday life—my deafness, to most people, even children, needs to be healed, mended, or fixed. I have to admit, however, that one of the delights of working with young children is listening to some of the darndest things they say. Katie, a talkative second-grader, with long blonde hair tied up in a ponytail and wearing sturdy glasses with purple frames, sat down with me one day to begin her reading session. Because I had just met Katie, I explained to her in terms that most second-graders could grasp that I am deaf, which meant that my ears do not work and that I do not hear at all. This young lady, all of six or seven years old, going on twenty-seven, made clear to me that there are many remedies for hearing loss. Katie, with one finger wagging skyward, began with the fact that she hopes to be a doctor when she grows up.

Katie's first course of action for my little problem was to get that special thing that deaf people can stick in their ears to help them hear better. Most of them are brown or tan, but sometimes they come in bright colors. She noted that I should get a pink one, because the boy in her class has a green one. When I mentioned those "things" are called hearing aids, she waved her hand and went yakking on. Next, Katie suggested I should try the stuff that "machine-people" make to stick inside one's brain. They would drill a hole in my skull while I was sleeping, and then when I wake up, I would hear again. But if that doesn't work, Katie continued, there is pink medicine. I could drink it down like strawberry milk. It absolutely must be taken before bedtime, so that after the medicine goes down my throat, I'm lying down immediately, and the medicine would travel back up to my ears and soak them. When I wake up in the morning, I would be able to hear again.

The next morning, however, I woke up still deaf. As I settled in at my desk with a cup of orange juice and a granola bar, a colleague marched into my office, wagged her finger back and forth, and announced loudly, "Meeting, no!" Of course, I had no idea what she was talking about. She kept repeating herself, enunciating in a wildly exaggerated manner, as if I was incapable of understanding a clarification or even a longer phrase. "Meeting, no! Meeting, no!" I was scrambling to ask specific questions: What meeting are we talking about? Was a meeting cancelled? Or was there no meeting scheduled that needed to be? Finally, she stormed out in exasperation, and I was left with understanding only two words and nothing else. Later in the day, I approached her and requested that she talk to me in full sentences about the meeting. Instead, she rattled off a litany of things, such as medication, surgery, hearing aids, cochlear implants, or even stem cell treatment, which I should be seeking to cure my hearing loss. And I still had no information about the mystery meeting. I was certainly amused by the recommendations of my prodigious second-grade otolaryngologist, but I tire of people almost daily providing counsel on what to do about my "problem."

Too often, persons with disabilities are seen as needing to be cured, to overcome obstacles, or in some cases, to get out of the way. Not only that, they are seen through the lens of what they *can't do* as opposed to what they *can do*, so interactions are liable to be watered down, patronizing, or condescending. Furthermore, many people make assumptions rather than politely ask how to facilitate a conversation or transaction. When people oversimplify when speaking to me, like my colleague did, I actually understand less. Some people talk to me in impossibly simplistic forms that could mean almost anything in the world. Some talk to me in longer sentences, but then they talk very slowly and exaggerate their mouth movements, making it much more difficult for me to lipread. Some will gesture wildly or try to remember some of the sign language they learned back in middle school. And some people, much to the annoyance of some of my family members or close friends, will talk very loudly at me. Speaking loudly certainly doesn't work either; I don't hear anything in the first place.

It is quite amusing how often I can lipread a person talking to someone else better than the same person talking to me. I might not catch all of the conversation, but it is usually a lot easier. And alas, there are some who won't even speak to me at all. They'll either say, "Never mind" and scurry off, or they will speak with whomever happens to be with me at the moment and totally ignore me. After stating that I'm deaf, that I can speak, and that I can lipread full sentences when a person is facing me, I always want to carry on with the conversation. Unfortunately, like many hearing people of different ethnicities, races, languages, and abilities, they frequently ask me to explain myself. The most common questions asked of me are where I am from; if I was born deaf; why I am deaf; if my parents are deaf; if I can drive a car, read a book, or have sex; why I didn't learn sign language . . . and why no one could cure my hearing. And quite often, many of my answers are either unheard or blatantly unaccepted in the end.

* * *

My maternal grandfather, whom I affectionately called *Grandad,* was the first to suspect my hearing loss. Short and stocky in stature, he was a gentle, knowing soul, who had delivered hundreds of babies as a well-respected and beloved obstetrician. Grandad insisted that my parents find a place to test my hearing, even though I was not quite three years old, and other physicians had told my parents to wait until I was at least six years old. That's how I found myself in a soundproof booth at a university research hospital. An audiometric exam involves wearing a set of headphones connected to an audiometer through which the audiologist methodically and precisely delivers sounds of varying tones and intensity to one ear at a time. The audiologist then plots and graphs on an audiogram the listener's response to the loudness of each tone.

Aside from my family bringing home our first puppy, this experience was one of my earliest memories, for there were stuffed animals bordering the window, not unlike at a carnival, between the examiner's room and the soundproof booth. It also had puppets for me to indicate whether I heard a sound through one or the other of my ears. Oftentimes, children and adults who hear sounds for the first time in their lives are overwhelmed with emotion; but for whatever reason, I have no recollection of this. I only remember being in awe of all the colorful stuffed rabbits, sheep, kittens, and puppies. It turned out that I had a 90-decibel hearing loss in both ears, meaning that sounds need to be as loud or louder than a jackhammer within a few feet of me for me to hear.

Otherwise, I could not, and still don't, hear much of anything. I suppose my parents were not terribly surprised at the results of the audiometric exam; it only confirmed their suspicion.

Next was a visit to an otolaryngologist, of which I have no recall, to determine the cause of my hearing loss. The ear is quite a sophisticated organ. The ear consists of three main parts: the outer ear, middle ear, and inner ear. The outer ear is the visible portion of the ear that collects sound waves and channels them into the ear canal. In the middle ear, the vibrations from the ear drum set three tiny bones called the *malleus* (hammer), *incus* (anvil), and *stapes* (stirrup) into motion, which in turn amplify and transfer sound to the inner ear. The Eustachian tube, also in the middle ear, is responsible for equalizing the pressure between the air outside the ear to that within the ear. Finally, the sound waves enter the inner ear and into the cochlea, a snail-shaped organ filled with fluid and nerve endings. The cochlea transforms the vibrations into electrical impulses that then travel along the auditory nerve to the brain. The brain then interprets these signals as sounds, and this is how we hear.

There are many causes and types of hearing loss, some of which are treatable and temporary, whereas others are permanent but can be managed. A *conductive hearing loss* can occur when there are problems with the outer ear, ear canal, ear drum, or the middle ear structures. Conductive hearing loss can result from varied causes, such as fluids in the middle ear from colds, ear infections, allergies, perforated ear drums, impacted earwax, or foreign objects in the ear. This type of hearing loss can also be found at birth due to malformation or dysfunction of the ear structures. *Sensorineural hearing loss* occurs when there are nerve-related problems of the inner ears. Such a hearing loss can be found at birth, or it can occur anytime during a person's lifespan due to exposure to loud noises, head trauma, virus or disease, genetics, aging, tumors, and malformation of the inner ear. It turned out that I have a sensorineural loss, one that I was born with. Although there are several theories, we don't know, and probably never will know, exactly what caused it.

After my diagnosis, my parents planned to do everything they could to bring me up as a *normal* child—that is, like a child who could hear. I was fitted with a hearing aid, which back then, was an archaic device about the size of a cigarette pack that I wore on a harness. A coil ran from the hearing aid to an ear mold inserted into my ear and provided me the input of sound. I was able to hear only loud noises and some voices at a close range but no speech sounds. I still needed to lipread most of the time. I have never ever heard the sound of singing birds, croaking frogs, wind blowing through the trees, higher notes of the piano and the flute, and dripping water. Even though hearing aids, as well as cochlear implants, have become more technologically sophisticated over the years, they are still incapable of perfectly correcting any hearing loss. It is not akin to putting on a pair of glasses and being able to see clearly again.

Hearing aids amplify quieter sounds and yet at the same time, compress louder sounds (so that they don't damage the ears), but there is inherent distortion. Hearing aids and cochlear implants do not cure hearing losses; they only offer the input of sound. Therefore, adjusting to wearing hearing aids or recovering from cochlear implants can be a difficult process for children and especially adults. Because I was a bit older than most children today when I received my first hearing aid, it was apparently quite an adjustment for me. While attending an early intervention program at a nearby university laboratory school, I threw my brand-new, and undoubtedly expensive for such young parents, hearing aid into the bushes in frustration. As I sat and pouted on the vast lawn of the campus, my mother, who was called, along with my teachers, the principal, several custodians, and many university students passing by stopped to search for it. I don't remember exactly why I threw my hearing aid, but I certainly remember how my pout gave away to fascination that I could garner such a reaction to my misbehavior. To my parents' relief, the search was successful, and I had to keep wearing the aid until I finally got used to it.

As I grew up, I was subjected to frequent hearing checks, so visits to the audiologists' offices became routine for me. Most times, I would wait patiently until I heard a sound and pressed the button, over and over again. Some days, I would press the button to try to hurry it along. Other days, I would try to fool the audiologist and get her all mixed up. The audiologist would try to determine what sounds I could hear, both with and without my hearing aids, and also what spoken words I could understand. The audiologist would cover her mouth with her hand in order to keep me from lipreading her and say compound words, such as *airplane, hotdog,* and *cowboy.* I had to try to repeat the words back to her. I consistently failed this portion of the exam, that is, until one time, an audiologist used the very list of words to shield her mouth. The list was backlit through the thick soundproof window, so I was able to read the entire list, albeit backwards, and remembered most of the words for future appointments.

For unknown reasons, I am no longer able to tolerate my hearing aids as an adult. Because I'm functioning well enough, I have no desire to undergo invasive surgery and intensive rehabilitation for a cochlear implant. Contrary to the news media, the promise of stem cell research and tissue engineering is still a long way off. Ultimately, simply fitting a hearing aid or even surgically implanting a cochlear implant and sending a person on his or her way is far from a cure.

People of all ages, including my second-grade otolaryngologist, are naturally curious about my deafness. It's not every day that they meet someone who has no hearing whatsoever. Some demand an explanation, and others are truly empathetic and want to understand. In every act of listening, questioning is absolutely central. Questions, interruptions, and even shifts to new questions occur while listening for ideas, information, and even new and challenging perspectives in order to determine whether one's belief should be retained, rejected, or modified. It is for this reason that I am more than willing to *explain* myself. I feel it is a civic and moral duty in our democratic country for all of us to share and to be open to diverse viewpoints, ethnicities, languages, and abilities. However, questions that come from people carrying deficit mind-sets about other people who are different from them tend to be stereotypical, judgmental, and even inflammatory. The underlying thought behind such questions is "What is wrong with you?" And then if I choose to engage in this conversation, it often ends with the attitude that although something is still "wrong" with me, I am "amazing" for overcoming my "problem." Admittedly, this gets old, and I would prefer to carry on with the conversation that was going to happen before it was found out that I was deaf. I certainly would like to find out more about the mystery meeting rather than be on the receiving end of a long-winded diatribe about curing my ears.

Unfortunately, the deficit mind-set reveals why some people won't listen to me when I try to explain how it is best for me to communicate with them. I explain that I can lipread and speak and that there is no need for shouting, exaggeration, or oversimplification. But because I am seen as having a deficit, I am also seen as unable to advocate for myself. I started out my life as a little terror, and to this day, I am still chastised for *not listening* when I simply did not *hear.* Furthermore, it is often insinuated that I am not upholding my responsibility to cure my deafness. I have been told numerous times that I have not come to terms with my hearing loss because of the requests I make for better communication, but the reality is that other people have not accepted my hearing loss. Simply put, communication is a two-way street, and it requires all parties to listen on a mutual level. Thus, a key piece of compassionate communication is learning how to listen fully with warmth, mindfulness, and openness in order to allow all of us to seek, query, question, debate, challenge, and even dispute, as we learn about multiple languages, linguistics, and literacies and expand our worldviews.

CAT AND MOUSE

MANY PEOPLE assume that because I am deaf and an educator, I work only with children who are deaf. The reality is that I work in public schools with diverse children from all walks of life, most of whom are hearing. I come across a child with a hearing loss about once every five years or so. Even though I could count the number of these children on one hand, I can deeply relate to their desires and challenges for listening, belonging, and learning. Zack, an energetic kindergartener with dark tousled hair and inquisitive eyes, was having a hard time during his small-group literacy sessions. Even though he had a mild hearing loss in one ear and a moderate loss in the other, he was an extroverted child and quickly made many friends in his first year of school. The administration asked me to observe him and see what kinds of strategies I could provide for his teacher, Mr. Byers, and his aide, Ms. Lee.

Every morning, Mr. Byers signaled "Reading Time" by putting on a pair of stuffed fox ears and calling his color-coded groups to his table for their literacy lessons. When his fox ears were atop his slightly balding head, the other children rotating around in centers were not to interrupt his group. Zack and three of his classmates were in the yellow group. Zack sat at the end of the horseshoe table, with Ms. Lee sandwiched between him and his three peers, so that Ms. Lee could be available to help Zack. Mr. Byers presented a book, called *Uncle Buncle's House*, containing a simple pattern with lively illustrations that any kindergartner could catch on and read along. Mr. Byers started reading aloud the first page, "There are seven clocks in Uncle Buncle's house." Zack, thoroughly interested, stood up, so he could see the book past Ms. Lee. Ms. Lee wagged a finger at Zack and reminded him to sit down. The other three children were sitting on their chairs, but the book was right in front of them. Mr. Byers continued reading, "There are six dogs in Uncle Buncle's house."

After a few moments of sitting, Zack stood up again, this time with one knee on the table, and leaned over so he could see. Ms. Lee turned and noticed that Zack was standing up again. She gently nudged Zack back to his seat and reminded him to sit down. But by this time, the other three children were standing, excitedly chiming in with the teacher reading the pattern book, "There are three gorillas . . ." Ms. Lee couldn't help but get caught up with the enthusiasm, and her back was turned to Zack. Then Zack sneaked up and crawled on top of the table past Ms. Lee to try to join the group. When Ms. Lee noticed Zack right next to her but atop the table, she berated Zack and reminded him for the third time to stay in his seat. Zack slouched back to his seat and pouted for a moment. He glanced behind him where they were reading the last page. "But there is only ONE Uncle Buncle!" Zack saw everyone laughing all around, but he was left out. Zack jumped up from his chair and angrily kicked the book bin on the floor beside the teacher's feet, scattering the books everywhere. Then he ran out of the classroom to one of his favorite hiding spots between a cabinet and a couch in an empty room. Both Mr. Byers and Ms. Lee looked at me with exasperation and simply asked, "See?"

Yes, I saw. From Zack's perspective. Zack was expected to sit in his chair, but he couldn't see the book past Ms. Lee. And he couldn't hear. To him, Ms. Lee was a physical wall between him and his peers. Zack's futile attempt to be part of reading the book with Mr. Byers and his peers was viewed as misbehavior. Although Mr. Byers believed in the concept of inclusion and was more than willing to have Zack in his classroom, he wasn't paying much attention to Zack, because he left it up to Ms. Lee, as an aide, to facilitate his participation. And Ms. Lee was keenly focused on helping Zack put on his best behavior, so that he could continue to be a part of his general education classroom despite his disability. After all, succeeding at school, for many children, means having to suppress their own identities and abilities and act within a narrowly defined and institutionalized view of what it means to be a *good student*. Although I was observing Zack, my memory flashed back to the first and only time I was sent to a principal's office for a similar offense. In my senior year!

I had eagerly looked forward to taking a humanities course. This class, offered only to seniors, was a sought-after advanced-placement class co-taught by four teachers in the auditorium. One had to have good academic standing in order to be accepted into this course. I had already taken a college course at our local university as a dual-enrolled student over the summer and knew the potential rigors of this class. We were going to cover literature, art, music, theater, philosophy, religion, and history. I couldn't wait! Alas, one of the teachers, Mrs. Chapman, upon finding out that I was deaf, called my mother and made it clear that I could not take the class. When my mother asked why not, the simple answer was because I couldn't hear, and it was just impossible for a deaf person to take on such an ambitious class. My mother hung up the telephone after stating that I now had every legal right to take this class and was perfectly capable of taking on this challenge.

On the first day of class, I entered the auditorium armed with note-paper and carbon paper (to stick under my friend's notepaper) and sat in the middle row off to the side, so that I could see the overhead projection, the teachers, and my peers during the lectures and discussions. Mrs. Chapman publicly demanded that I sit in the front row in the seat right in front of her. I was resistant, because after years of adapting to my hearing loss, I knew I was in the best viewing spot for listening. When she threatened to send me to the principal's office for being insubordinate, I dutifully got up and sat where she wanted me. It was as if a dark shell had been placed over my head. I could not lipread her, because the projector cart was in the way. I did not have willing, empathetic, and mature peers on either side of me who allowed me to check their notes. And I was scolded for scanning my textbooks in my attempts to try to keep up in the presentation instead of "listening" to her.

After class, I firmly explained to Mrs. Chapman why it was best for me to sit in the spot that I had originally chosen. She relented and allowed me to sit where I preferred; but for the next two weeks, she kept a vigilant eye on me. Of course, this made me keep a vigilant eye on her! The whole scenario became a ridiculous game of Cat and Mouse. I needed to juggle a lot of lipreading and taking notes, and yet she expected me to constantly look at her to demonstrate that I was listening. So, whenever she was not looking my way, I quickly jotted things down. Finally, one day, I got caught. I had missed a statement or two and happened to be looking over my friend's notes to find out what was said.

My friend kindly pointed at her notepaper to show me what I had just missed and empathetically smiled at me. The next thing I knew, a hall pass was placed in my hand, and I was immediately sent to the principal's office in trouble for not listening.

Zack and I, both having hearing losses, were trying to be part of our educational community, one that was in a hearing world. Zack had climbed on the horseshoe table to see past his aide. I needed to have full view in my humanities course by sitting on the side of the auditorium. Instead, we were disciplined for not listening, misbehaving, or otherwise being insubordinate. Indeed, Zack was powerless and angry. Thus, he stormed out of the classroom. Although I felt hurt and angry too, I knew that I was being set up to fail the humanities course. I knew that if the teachers wouldn't accept me, and if I couldn't change their minds, then I needed to leave as well. Because I was older and more mature, I came to understand that it was a poor reflection on them, not on me. I also knew that if I wanted to graduate on time, I'd best not take on this battle to assert my rights. Lamentably, although this was a well-deserved opportunity for me, I also knew it was a lost cause. It was not a matter of giving up myself but of a teacher giving up on me before I even had a chance to prove myself. Ultimately, it turned out that I had enough credits to take just one last course of my public school career, which was an advanced-placement literature course, and I walked out of that high school graduating a semester earlier than my peers. Zack, on the other hand, needed my advocacy.

Although the phrase of *good* listening is rather easy, offering a clear idea of what that involves is more elusive. Many people, including Ms. Lee and Mrs. Chapman, assumed that being a good listener meant sitting quietly and looking directly at the adult. Because it takes intense concentration for me to lipread and comprehend, I can easily come across to some as a good or a caring listener in a one-on-one conversation. I always try to listen with warmth, so that hopefully I don't come across as aggressive with a seemly steely stare. Additionally, I need others to look directly at me when I'm talking, for it provides me feedback as to how my speech and volume is coming across to them. However, such behaviors of eye contact are not always the best condition for listening. Eye contact is a culturally influenced nonverbal behavior. In some cultures, direct eye contact is considered rude or threatening, and in other cultures, speakers may see people listening with their eyes shut, because it is thought to facilitate listening. Children's conversational and discourse rules, such as turn-taking, interrupting, use of silence, and so forth, are largely determined not only by cultural rules, but also by the social rules of their interactions with adults. The ways that both children and adults listen are culturally, socially, and deeply ingrained, but unfortunately, are too often met with indifference. All people, including Zack and myself, have multiple ways of listening, including interrupting, asking questions, and deferring our reactions. And we show many different types of nonverbal listening behaviors, including eye contact, the amount of interpersonal space we use, our body language, how we touch one another, and even the use of gestures. In Zack's case, it also involved climbing on the table.

Furthermore, teaching that is directive in nature—by giving information, asking questions, giving directions, making assignments, monitoring seat work, reviewing assignments, giving and reviewing tests, assigning and reviewing homework, settling disputes, punishing noncompliance, and giving grades rather than encouraging interaction—does not work in our schools. A classroom atmosphere created by constant teacher direction and student compliance seethes with passive resentment that sometimes bubbles up into overt resistance, especially in schools with diverse populations. Mr. Byers, however, conducted his literacy sessions in a delightfully authentic and purposeful manner. He used a captivating book as the basis for learning phonics, sight words, syntax, and comprehension. At one point, even his three students were standing, and even jumping a bit, but they were enthusiastic and fully engaged in their literacy learning. Mrs. Chapman was teaching a world of literature, art, music, theatre, philosophy, religion, and history. But Zack and I, for the sole reasons that we had a disability, were unwittingly excluded from class participation because of our "noncompliance." Our teachers had different expectations for our behavior than they had for other students. Zack couldn't get closer to the book, but his peers were standing, some even excitedly jumping up and down. I couldn't sit with my peers, who knew me and allowed me to peek at their notes in order to follow the presentation.

Teachers and bosses who dictate the environment invariably exclude some of their students and employees. People of all ethnicities, races, languages, and abilities experience exclusion in many forms, both overt and covert. It creates a sense of "us versus them," and the expectations, usually gauged against mainstream norms and standards, become unreasonable, inequitable, and unfair. Zack should have been given the opportunity to switch seats with Ms. Lee or otherwise, move closer to the book, and I should have been allowed to look over at my peers' notes. Thus, I am dead serious when I insist that it is not just Zack and I who are deaf, but it is *all* of us who must *listen*.

THE HELP

MOST PEOPLE appreciate receiving help; however, helping people who have health issues or disabilities, even when well-meaning, can be inadvertently detrimental rather than supportive. Brady, who was short and skinny for his age and had a headful of red hair, struggled with depression in middle school and was thought to be a danger to himself. A aide followed him everywhere, from the cab that dropped him off, to all of his classes, and into the bathrooms, to make sure he was always safe. This aide, who had recently retired from an executive position and enjoying a second career helping out in schools, was always three to five steps behind Brady. The aide even talked to his teachers and carried his books for him.

Emma, a friendly third-grader with quadriplegia, was perpetually in a circular wall of teacher assistants, a full-time nurse, and one or two of her therapists, all of whom dutifully attended to her needs. Frequently, the adults chatted among themselves while they surrounded Emma in her wheelchair. Emma was always in the back of her classroom, last in line, and alone at lunch and recess, apart from her peers.

Sydney, exuberant and outgoing, was in fifth grade, but due to a learning disability, she read three years below grade level. Whenever Sydney's classmates had academic instruction in reading, writing, or mathematics, a community or parent volunteer, a high school tutor, or a classroom aide took Sydney out into the hallway to learn phonics on worksheets or to practice words from flash cards. Sometimes she was allowed to draw pictures or listen to a story. Other times, even to her delight, she and an adult would do odd jobs for the teacher, such as tracing and cutting out colorful leaves for the classroom bulletin board.

Although Brady, Emma, and Sydney all had different health issues or disabilities, all three of them had helpers in the form of assistant teachers, aides, and even volunteers. The goal was to include them in mainstream classrooms but ultimately, they were there only in body, not fully included, learning, or growing among their peers. They each ended up

on invisible islands of their own. Brady complained about being followed constantly. He protested that he "couldn't shake off the guy with
the stupid tie." He even remarked it was embarrassing enough to be
short and skinny with red hair, but the guy following him was making his depression worse. Emma was sad because she "didn't have any
friends in her school." No one her age talked to her. Sydney pointed out
bitterly that she hadn't learned multiplication, even though it was on a
state standardized test and asked, "Why should I be tested on something
I haven't even learned yet?" All three received adult assistance for safety
or academic reasons based on the decisions of their individualized educational planning teams. Even though the decisions, and the help, were
made in good faith, no one heard the words of Brady, Emma, or Sydney.
This is not to say that the students didn't need help, but the quality of
their inclusion, access to academic opportunities, and educational experiences were inadvertently diminished and even isolating for them.

Because I was in school long before laws were passed to protect my
educational rights, I never had assistance or accommodations. I had to
figure out things my own way. Yet, I was still isolated from not hearing
the talk among my teacher and peers. I tried reminding my teachers to
face my way, so that I could lipread. I sat on the edge of the classroom,
instead of right up in the front, so that I could try to lipread my peers
too. And I did constant reminding. Many teachers paced back and forth
while lecturing. Many continued talking while turning their backs to
write on the chalkboard. Although the visual information on the screen
pulled down in front of the chalkboard was helpful, the overhead projector almost always blocked my view of the teacher. If a student asked a
question or a comment without raising his or her hand, I always missed
it. And if someone did raise a hand, other students were in my way for
me to lipread as well. Many times, I gave up reminding people and trying to keep up, because I had it in the back of my mind that if I was considered an annoyance, difficult, or even uneducable, I could find myself
kicked out of school.

Most people would say things have changed and that one can never
step in the same river twice. By the same token, one can't go home again.
On two occasions, however, I returned to childhood locations that I

expected to find changed, but then found things eerily the same as they were before. When we first moved to my childhood neighborhood, the trees lining the streets were mere saplings. When I visited as an adult, the houses hadn't changed much, but all of the trees had grown large, and the streets were dappled and shady. Then, at my last visit, the trees were saplings again! Invasive beetles had wiped out all of the original trees, and the entire neighborhood was replanted again. It was a jarring experience.

As a child, I loved to skate at the university ice arena, which was converted from an athletic field house to a hockey rink. The set of tall windows running both lengths of the building provided bright and natural light. When I returned as a young adult, I found all the windows boarded up, apparently as the result of vandalism or the fact that the streaming sunlight was melting the ice. I continued to skate there, and one year after major renovations, including the installation of new windows, I found myself right back at my childhood rink. So, I wasn't sure what to expect when I arrived at my junior high school, now a middle school, for a morning classroom observation and an afternoon meeting in my role as a literacy consultant. As a junior high school student, I had intimate knowledge of the physical surroundings of my former classrooms, from the brushed gray knobs and pulls on the wooden cabinets to the white ceiling tiles to the steel bracket on top of the wooden doors to keep them from slamming. I had plenty of time to pretend I was listening, for I noticed that other students listen without necessarily looking at the teacher or each other. I constantly sought written information about the lectures—on the chalkboard, from the overhead projector, in handouts, and books—but when none were available (which was most of the time), I counted the number of tiles on the ceiling. Then I counted the number of tiles on the floor. I counted the number of desks in rows. I counted the number of students. When tired of counting, I looked at everyone's shoes—platform shoes, earth shoes, western boots, two-toned shoes, and Vans. Then I wondered why anyone would want to wear bell-bottom jeans. They seemed to me as quite noisy and dirty, swishing between the legs and dragging on the floor.

If a critter moved across the floor, it would receive my intense interest. A spider? An ant? A small beetle? I was tempted to pull my book out of my backpack to read, but I feared that I would get in trouble for not listening to the lecture. Therefore, when I walked into my old English classroom to observe the current learning environment, I noticed that the chalkboard was replaced by a whiteboard and there was new furniture, but the same teacher's wooden desk was in the same back corner of the room. The brown cabinets and the gray knobs and pulls, white ceiling tiles, beige floor tiles, and steel bracket on the door were still there. The view out the window hadn't changed, and I suspected that the cobweb in the corner of the window was the ancestral home for a long lineage of spiders. Of course, my teachers had retired, and the students were of a new generation.

For this classroom observation, I had a captioner by my side. Communication Access Realtime Translation (CART) is a method of speech-to-text translation, like captions on television. A CART provider, using a stenographic machine, laptop computer, and real-time software, listens to and transcribes every word, so that it can be read on the computer almost as soon as it is spoken. The captions can be read on a personal laptop, even remotely over the internet, or projected on a large screen for a larger audience. The Americans with Disabilities Act now recognizes CART as an assistive technology that provides effective access to communication. CART services have become one of the most requested accommodations, both in schools and workplaces, for individuals with hearing losses who do not use ASL interpreters. I can see why. With fast keystrokes and sophisticated software programs, CART specialists have made a huge difference in my ability to access announcements, lectures, and discussions.

The teacher I observed was using a short murder mystery in order to teach the specific vocabulary and concepts needed to discuss the genre, such as *alibi, deduction, red herring, sleuth, suspect,* and *motive*. The students had many different comments and questions about the mystery, until they finally figured out that a butler was lying about inserting a note between pages 77 and 78 of a book left on an old desk. Odd and even numbered pages are always on the front and back of the same sheet of paper, making it impossible to insert a note in between the pages. Although it took a little bit of practice to read the six or eight lines of captions on the laptop screen and jot notes, it was definitely easier than attempting to lipread the teacher who was constantly on the move around the front of the classroom or the volley of conversations among the students. I was able to read how the teacher intentionally used the vocabulary of the genre among the students, such as asking them to think about red herrings in the mystery. The various responses were delightful, revealing characteristics of the students themselves and their diverse backgrounds, and some comments even led to further conversations about defining *non sequitur* and citing *evidence*. What a huge difference in the quality of my experience as compared to my junior high school years!

Although technology has come a long way, much progress needs to be done on how we think about helping people who appear to be vulnerable. There is a difference between assistance that maintains the status quo of disability and dependence versus accommodations that foster ability and independence. When people try to assist me, *they* are the ones making the decisions as to what I should or would like to hear. Even when I sense that I am missing something and ask other people, it is ultimately up to them as to whether or not they are in a position to or willing to fill in my gaps. On the other hand, when using accommodations like CART, *I* am the one who chooses what information I want to attend to or even whether or not I want to tune out altogether. However, despite the benefits of CART, I find I am treated differently at conferences or meetings, where there is an in-person CART provider versus remote CART service over the internet. A CART provider sitting by my side with a stenographic machine reveals my disability, sometimes physically isolating me from my colleagues and reducing other people's expectations of my professional capabilities. Whereas, sitting at a conference table using remote captioning with just my laptop in front of me, makes me look and interact like everyone else.

When providing assistance to a person with a disability or difference, we must be mindful of her or his physical separation from the mainstream, unnecessary dependence, interference with peer interaction, feelings of stigmatization, limited access to instruction and discussions, and even loss of personal control. CART has allowed me to listen to differing perspectives on topics as well as contribute appropriately to the discussions. It also allowed me to be amused by the numerous quips and humorous exchanges among the students and my colleagues in the moment, not at a later time when it was no longer as funny. Instead of counting things in the classrooms and boardrooms and looking at the variety of everyone's shoes, I was finally able to observe and *listen* to lessons and meetings. I felt much more independent, intelligent, articulate, and confident instead of scrambling around to comprehend and fill in gaps. Now this was what it seemed like to *hear*!

PART 3

SPEAKING

INTRODUCTION: DEFINING SPEAKING

Out of the mouth of babes.

—PSALMS

IN ITS SIMPLEST form, speaking can be viewed as the articulation of sounds and words. Although it is helpful to be intelligible, this definition is limited. Speaking also is an act of sharing, conveying thoughts, and expressing ourselves. Forms of expression can be made not only during conversations and public speaking, but also in art, music, and movement . . . and in sign language. Using sign language is a form of speaking as well, in that the signer conveys words and ideas. Speaking is not only delivered through words, but also in tone of voice, mannerisms, mood, aura, and appearances. Deaf and hard of hearing people are astutely tuned to multiple forms of expression, whether spoken or not. For some deaf and hard of hearing people, the ability to be understood is a bigger struggle than the issue of hearing loss itself. Their voices and the way they pronounce some words may sound different, and they may have difficulty modulating their volume with respect to the ambient noise. Thus, deaf people who are speaking need hearing people to face them so they can monitor for feedback and understanding. All of us, deaf and hearing, benefit from watching a speaker's expressions and body language, and even by lipreading. Our potential to speak and express ourselves is mutually tied to how well others are willing to listen.

FONTS AND ELOCUTION

SPEAKING IS an emotionally laden endeavor. Public speaking can be nerve wracking for many people. Self-expression to meet an emotional or physical need or desire can result in an argument or passion among family members, friends, and lovers. And articulation—accents and dialects—can give way to judgment of one's culture, intelligence, character, or personal worth. In my case, my credentials—my education, experience, expertise, and published works—often get questioned with skepticism the moment I open my mouth and speak.

* * *

Tonya, a young first-grader, was feeling timid and self-conscious when I asked her to read a page from a book to me, but my warmth and reassurance won her over. However, after a few moments, Spencer, one seat over, became increasingly exasperated that Tonya wasn't saying anything. Over and over, he exclaimed, "But she's NOT saying anything! She's not saying anything!" To me, Tonya seemed to be reading just fine. Now, Spenser was a third-grade kid who regularly goofed off, so I, only slightly bemused by his insistence, gently reminded him to read his own book. I returned to lipreading Tonya reading another page out of her book while taking a running record. Running records are a method of observing and coding the accuracy, omissions, errors, self-corrections, and commentaries children make as they read aloud a short passage. These notes are later reviewed for making individualized instructional decisions and planning the next reading lesson. However, because reading aloud takes on a different cognitive load than reading silently, I take running records only for a paragraph or a few short pages at a time, just enough to provide me with an adequate picture of my students' current strengths and weaknesses in reading. After all, proficient and fluent readers are not exact word-by-word readers. And even adults who read aloud may change a few words without necessarily changing the meaning of words or phrases.

Reading is by far not a linear activity, but a nonlinear process where proficient readers can read ahead a bit and then go back when something needs clarification. The whole point of reading is to deepen our understanding and comprehension of texts, not to just read the words perfectly. Thus, for many people of all ages, reading aloud for performance (as opposed to sharing, such as a bedtime story) can be a cumbersome and anxiety-provoking activity.

It wasn't until later that I figured out what was up with Spenser. One day, my daughter, Kara, stopped by my school while she was between college classes and decided to watch me teach reading. At the time, I had a group of three third-grade boys, including Spenser, in my office. In the process of observing, Kara became puzzled, because Jeremy, who was supposed to be reading aloud, wasn't saying anything. Although I looked and sounded normal as I was working with Jeremy, something was not right to her. Kara looked at me, and then she stooped down to look at Jeremy. She looked at me again and then looked at the Jeremy again. She started to say something to me, but I winked at her, indicating that I knew Jeremy had made an error in his reading but wanted to wait and see if he discovered that on his own. Kara looked at Jeremy again, rolled her eyes, and decided to tell me later. At dinner that evening, Kara told me that Jeremy was not making any sound at all. He was mouthing the words as he read along to me, and I was responding to him as if he were reading aloud! Of course, being deaf, I had no idea. When I asked Jeremy about it the next day, he just shrugged his shoulders and commented that he did that all the time, because he didn't want his classmate Spenser to hear him. And the next time I saw Tonya, she admitted that she discovered that I could understand her without her using her voice. With great relief, she explained it was so that Spenser wouldn't hear her reading either and taunt her behind my back. Although I wised up to this particular situation, over time, I found that many of my students, including a few high school students, who struggle with reading, discover and feel safer reading "aloud" to me by mouthing the words silently.

Many people consistently hear the terms *speech* and *language* paired together as one concept. However, language is different from speech. Language is made up of socially shared rules that include the use of word meanings and what word combinations and phrases are best used in what situations. It can include body language, written language, multiple languages, and even sign language. Speech, on the other hand, is the verbal means of communicating and consists of articulation, voice, and fluency. Although some people with developmental disabilities, cognitive impairments, or traumatic brain injuries, as well as people who have had a stroke, can have speech and/or language issues, it is easy to forget that most people with speech disorders, deaf people, and even people with different accents have perfectly normal intelligence and capabilities.

Unfortunately, speech is an easy medium for teasing, mocking, or constant correction. I can empathize with the anxiety that Tonya and Jeremy felt when Spencer was around, especially because I wasn't hearing Spencer's antics to stop his unacceptable behavior. For I too have experienced ridicule and prejudice because of my speech, one that is characteristic of deafness, and sometimes even to the point where I need someone else to stand up for me.

When I picked up Kevin, a serious and studious first-grader, from his classroom to begin his reading assessment, I discovered that he could not understand a word I was saying. He sat down and listened very attentively to me. At times, he was even inches from my face, turning his ear, and looking all puzzled. I asked Kevin if he could hear me, because I'm not always sure of my volume with respect to the ambient noise. Kevin responded that he was able to hear me, but that I talked funny. I explained that I spoke differently, because I don't hear, even though this is a difficult concept for most children at his age to grasp. Still, I kept talking, and Kevin was slowly beginning to get used to my speech. At one point, I asked Kevin if he had any rules at home for playing video games. He asked what I was saying about video games. I tried as hard as I could to enunciate my initial r sound in *rules*. Finally, I gave him examples of rules that some children have, such as playing for only an hour a day or only on weekends. After several attempts and examples, Kevin finally leaned back and exclaimed, "Oh, rules!"

Kevin's struggles to understand my speech gave me a clue that he had a tendency to focus on minute details rather than the bigger picture, and that he wasn't using contextual skills. When I reported this back to Mr. Taylor, his general education teacher, he retorted, "Well, I didn't think that many first-graders would be able to understand you anyway. You shouldn't be working in elementary schools, because of the way you talk. You're not setting a good example for the kids either." This was indeed frustrating, having to stand up for myself before I can advocate for my students. I explained that I've worked with hundreds of young children for many years. About once every three or four years, I'll come across a child who is like Kevin. In fact, I explained that my last one was a fifth-grader who insisted on correcting my speech rather than focusing on his literacy. In being humorous, I shared how I was actually getting free speech therapy from a kid!

No matter, Mr. Taylor's position was unchanged, and I was reported to the administrator of the school district as being unqualified for working with his student. Fortunately, the district administrator, knowing the depth and breadth of my expertise and capabilities, stood by me and told me to carry on with the assessment and continue with the eventual and necessary meetings. When I brought Kevin to my office the next day, I had him read several children's books. One of these books, *Good-Night Owl!*, contained a story about an owl trying to get some sleep (in the daytime!) while a variety of other birds and animals made a noisy racket all around. Kevin was able to name eleven kinds of creatures and the sounds they made, except for one. That one was a blue jay, a very common bird in our area. Kevin announced that he could not read the word *jay*, because he had never before seen that first letter. That particular *j* in the book was typeset in such a way that the letter did not have a curled tail. That letter just extended straight down, another tangible clue that Kevin focuses on small details in cognitively processing both oral language, such as my speech, as well as print in reading.

Even though my inner voice sighed, "Are we not done with 'standard' English, the elocution police, round robin reading, and a multitude of other judgments of what it means to be perfectly *articulate*?" I held my thoughts. Kevin was only in first grade. He had not likely had years of other people bidding him to be highly accurate in attending to speech and reading. Instead, I had to be mindful of how other people, including children, cognitively process language, literacies, and linguistics, just as I want people to understand what I have to do to communicate without hearing.

Of course, there is no need for such perfect accuracy, but Kevin, by nature, keenly focused on *phonemes* (letter sounds), such as the *r* in *rules* and the *j* in *blue jays*. I, on the other hand, am bedeviled with *visemes*, those phonemes that look a lot alike on the lips, such as (*m, b, p*), (*t, d*), and (*f, v*). Therefore, *homophenous* words (words that look alike when lipreading), such as *mat, bat*, and *pat*, are particularly vexing to lipreaders. I use content strategies to sort out words and phrases for comprehension in addition to lipreading sounds. For example, I know that my husband, family, and close friends are not saying *elephant juice* when they say, "I love you," even though these phrases look remarkably the same.

When I respond in a conversation, I have to formulate my speech, think about my pronunciations, adjust my volume, and deliver my message. Most people are using a balance of cues when listening—attention to details, the whole context, tone, body language—without much thought. Kevin and I, however, are on the extreme ends of this balance when listening to speakers. Kevin overly focuses on details, such as phonemes, and I manage my lipreading using both lexical (word) and contextual constraints to rule out possible words and lexical and contextual prediction to determine what makes most sense, along with being mindful of homophenous words.

The intense concentration for lipreading and speaking is exhausting. Put Kevin and me together in one room, and kindness and patience are certainly called for. And of course, neither of us would want Spenser or Mr. Taylor around. When I worked with Kevin for a while, I was able to teach him how to pull together lexical and contextual cues to support his reading by covering up every sixth or seventh word in a short passage and having him continue to read by filling in the blanks with words that would make sense. Of course, this instructional strategy encouraged Kevin to read ahead, return to the blanked-out word, and read for comprehension rather than letter by letter.

Just like the physiological phenomenon of hearing, the ability to speak, in which sound waves must make its way through the outer, middle, and inner ear of another person, is quite a marvel too. Before any sound can be produced at all, there has to be a source of energy. In speech, the energy takes the form of a stream of air, which in normal circumstances, is set in motion by the lungs. When we can speak, the air from the lungs has to be converted into audible vibrations. The larynx, the most important source of vibration, is a tube consisting of cartilages with connecting ligaments and membranes and within it there are two bands of muscular tissue known as the vocal folds. Once the air stream passes through the larynx, it enters the long tubular structure known as the vocal tract. Here the sound is affected by the action of several mobile organs, such as the tongue, soft palate, and lips, which work together to make a wide range of speech sounds. I offered only a snippet on the anatomy and physiology of speech, but indeed there are so many pieces that must be in place for us to speak. And there is a lot that can go wrong. Some people may stutter, have medical issues with their lungs or voices, or have apraxia, a disorder in which messages from the brain to the mouth are disrupted, or dysarthria, in which the speech muscles are weak.

Deaf and hard of hearing people are very aware that their speech is "different." They don't need to be told again and again that something is wrong with their speech or their reading. In fact, listeners who appear impatient or annoyed actually make it much harder for them to speak or read. Finishing sentences, filling in words, or telling speakers to slow down, relax, or take a deep breath is patronizing. Additionally, pointing out and correcting speech only serves to emotionally shut down conversations, because it becomes clear that enunciation is more important than the message. I don't mind being told how *caveat* or *Galapagos Islands* are actually pronounced, but please wait until I'm finished talking and then tell me only in a private time and space. During the conversation, it is much kinder to ask what I mean, so that I can come up with a different word or explanation. When I teach reading, I always wait until my students discover their miscues on their own or until they are at the end of the paragraph or book. And I save the lesson on their miscues for a private time and space. Ultimately, showing empathy and patience for listening to other people's messages is the life lesson that Spenser and Mr. Taylor need to learn and a virtue that all of us can strengthen.

BABY STUFF

EMOTIONAL OUTBURSTS or sullen silences can be a result of communication breakdowns. Many times, our first impulse is to pull away or demand that the temperamental person snap out of it, but what that person really needs is someone who listens well, without evaluation, judgment, or defensiveness. Of course, listening when there is a breakdown is hard to do. Skylar, a fourth-grade student, stormed past me and down the hall in anger, just as I arrived to his classroom to pick him up for reading intervention. He wove his way through the throng of students, stomping along and brushing their shoulders, with his arms folded against his chest. I glanced over to his teacher with a puzzled look on my face. Holding up a piece of paper as she worked her way around rows of desks, she met me at the door to explain that Skylar was having difficulty reading and comprehending the passage that was in her hand. She asked that I help Skylar with it. I glanced down the long hallway and saw that Skylar was kicking my locked office door in frustration. When I let Skylar in, he kicked a few chairs around and finally plopped down on a beanbag chair with a pout, not quite ready to talk yet.

This was my first year in Skylar's school building. Caseload numbers fluctuate from building to building and from year to year throughout the district. Thus, I had just moved into my new office on short notice. I hadn't had time yet to go over all of the student records. I was told that Skylar needed reading intervention because he had a speech and language disorder, learning disabilities, an attention deficit disorder, and was prone to outbursts. When Skylar was ready to talk, he explained that he read the passage, which was now in my hands, out loud to his teacher. Then his teacher wanted him to retell the passage. But Skylar became exasperated, because he had just read the passage to her. Skylar asked me what he was supposed to tell her. I chuckled and remarked that he had a good point. But I hadn't read the passage yet. Would he tell *me* about it? Even though he had some difficulty putting his sounds and words together in order and would stutter at times, Skylar explained the setting, who the characters were, what happened, and how it ended. It was obvious that he comprehended the passage. However, attempting to dig a little bit deeper, when I asked Skylar how he felt about the passage, his tone changed back to anger: "It's all baby stuff!" And he added, "Why everyone think I'm stuuu . . . pid? I read baby stuff then I'm s'pose to tell it. Makes no sense why." And then he returned to the beanbag chair, pouting again.

Indeed, the passage was marked at a first-grade level. And indeed, it was "baby stuff" for a fourth-grade boy. Skylar not only became a victim of his labels, but also because of the way he talked and read out loud. Here, we are reminded to distinguish between language itself and the deeply entrenched attitudes and stereotypes that most people hold about language. When a person speaks, conclusions are immediately drawn about that person's social class background, level of education, country of origin, and his or her intelligence and capabilities. Unfortunately, I have had many personal experiences with people deeming me unintelligent, uneducated, or illiterate, because my speech is characteristic of a deaf person. And I have seen children, like Skylar, who have a speech and language disorder, confront systemic judgments about their capabilities to learn. We ought to be aware of the power of such linguistic stereotyping. Skylar should have had the opportunity to discuss what he gained from the text from his perspective and worldviews, not simply to complete a reading assignment in which he reads out loud word by word and answers canned multiple-choice questions. To add to Skylar's woes, he was requested to read aloud and retell a passage far below his actual cognitive capabilities and interest level. From the adults around him, he was fully aware of the attitudes and lower expectations for him. Too often, when children are identified as *low-achieving*, they are more likely to be asked to read aloud, to have their attention focused on word recognition rather than comprehension, to spend more time working on low-level worksheets than on reading authentic texts, and to experience more fragmentation in their instructional activities. As in Skylar's words—*baby stuff*. Baby stuff is something I'm all too familiar with myself.

When my son, Keane, was a baby, he woke up from an afternoon nap with an alarmingly high fever. As any concerned mother would do,

I took him to the nearest urgent care center, where I was pleased to meet a physician with graying hair and a seemingly gentle disposition. As I was explaining that I was deaf and that I lipread, Dr. Thomas smiled at me, took Keane from my arms, placed him on the examining table, and wordlessly checked him from head to toe. Then Dr. Thomas pulled out a prescription pad from his white coat pocket, made a few scribbles, turned to me, and with exaggerated enunciation announced, "Your . . . baby . . . will . . . be . . . okay!" While pointing out the window with one hand and placing his prescription with his other hand into mine, he continued to exaggerate his enunciation: "Take . . . this . . . to . . . the . . . drug . . . store!" My first thought was that my son was the baby, not me. I didn't need to be talked to like a baby. I looked down at the prescription and startled Dr. Thomas by reading it aloud: "Bactrim." Then I said, "But Keane is allergic to sulfa-based drugs. The last time he took it, he turned blue. My mom, who was visiting at the time, and I rushed him to the hospital."

No matter, Dr. Thomas continued his attempts to assure me: "Your baby will be okay! Go to the drug store!" By this time, I was understandably indignant that Dr. Thomas wouldn't listen to me. He wouldn't listen to the fact that I could lipread and read. And he wouldn't listen to my concern about the prescription. He guided me out of the examining room, patting my hand: "He will be okay!" He might as well have patronizingly patted my head. When I arrived at the checkout desk, I fell into helpless tears. As I tried to explain to the clerk that Dr. Thomas prescribed a medication that Keane was allergic to, she rolled her eyes and told me not to worry: "The doctor knows what he is doing." Enraged, I left the clinic, carefully buckled Keane in his car seat, and drove over to the drugstore, with large fat tears rolling down my cheeks. Fortunately, the pharmacist listened, checked the database, and called the urgent care clinic for a different prescription. Needless to say, I never went back that urgent care clinic again.

Many disabilities, such as deafness, are not physically obvious. The people of distinguished authority, Skylar's teacher and Keane's doctor, were viewing Skylar and myself through the lens of our speech, speech that is different to the norm, and quickly made erroneous assumptions about our abilities to belong, function, comprehend, and contribute to the wider world. As an adult, I can make choices about who I interact with, what stores and businesses I frequent, and even what healthcare facilities I visit; however, Skylar was stuck in a school, where he had little say in his learning environment. Both of us have differences in our speech, and in my case, I am also deaf, but we are not babies, dumb, and or even illiterate. It is always obvious to us when we are subjected to pity or patronization. But what is not so clear is how to get ourselves out of such situations without being further victimized and exposed to the derogatory perception that we are angry, indigent, or even crazy.

Prior to 1975 (the year I turned thirteen), our schools, according to the U.S. Department of Education, "educated only one in five children with disabilities, and many states had laws excluding certain students, including children who were 'deaf, blind, emotionally disturbed, or mentally retarded.'" Martin, Martin, and Terman noted that until the mid-1970s, laws in most states even "allowed school districts to refuse to enroll any student they considered 'uneducable.'" (These were the terms used in that time.) The notion that children with deafness are "uneducable," began way back when Aristotle (384 B.C.–322 B.C.), a Greek philosopher, implied that deaf (as well as blind) people were incapable of being taught, of learning, or of reasoned thinking. Translated by G. R. G. Mure, Aristotle wrote that "the loss of any one of the senses entails the loss of a corresponding portion of knowledge, and that, since we learn either by induction or by demonstration, this knowledge cannot be acquired." Today, despite lingering issues of inequitable opportunities to learn in schools, we know that children with hearing losses or deafness are fully capable of developing language and literacy skills comparable of their hearing peers.

Since I was "somehow" educated and am now fully literate, there is a widespread perception that I must have been an extremely precocious child. This is not entirely true. Both Skylar and I are intelligent, but Skylar was on his way to becoming a victim of gaps in opportunity to learn in school. I was lucky, in that I was provided an opportunity for an education in a progressive community from preschool through college. I was lucky that, at the time, politicians and education policy makers didn't measure every step of my way with yearly standardized tests that I would have "failed" in the window of time it took me to catch up. Skylar, on the other hand, was being covertly segregated in resource rooms and reading low-level materials without having any voice in his learning.

Although there is little connection between speech and intelligence, we should be mindful of receptive-expressive language gaps. Simply put, *receptive language* is the receipt of a message aurally or visually, whereas *expressive language* is the conveyance of a message orally, manually, or graphically. However, less understood is the receptive-expressive language gap. We all, including young children, have passive knowledge of many aspects of our languages, words, and constructions, which we can understand but never actively use. We comprehend much more speech and language than we can actually use or speak ourselves. Most of us are able to perceive and understand linguistic distinctions, such as accents or grammatical forms, which we do not or cannot make ourselves. Although a discrepancy between receptive versus expressive language is a normal phenomenon for monolingual speakers, it is particularly more pronounced for bilingual speakers of all ages, those with speech and language disorders, and deaf and hard of hearing people. Skylar pointed out that he was reading baby books and felt that the adults around him thought of him as stupid, although he didn't entirely understand that it was an unfortunate outcome of his receptive-expressive language gap. In my case, I am able to understand, particularly through reading, much more than I am able to articulate, for I don't know how many words are pronounced. We must be cautious in equating the inability to *use* language with the ability to *understand* it. Therefore, listening requires mindfully avoiding assumptions and deficit views that there is something wrong with the speaker, mentally or emotionally.

Ontology deals with the nature of being. For example, researchers who study child development can take different ontological positions, about children as biologically immature humans; that is, they are inherently vulnerable and dependent upon adults for protection, they are an oppressed minority group, and they have their own culture, which is very different than that of adults. And different societies have different ideas about what children are, in that childhood is a cultural construction, not just a natural state. However, some researchers now argue that we should recognize children's agency (their ability to act on their own behalf) and their citizenship as human beings now and not just in the future, and we should involve children as the central research participants. They also suggest that when working with children, it is helpful to consider our own assumptions about childhood and youth, so that children are seen as active beings and not just passive recipients of parental or professional care. On that note, although most of us are not researchers, people who are educators, parents, employers, policy makers, and even physicians should be aware of their ontological approaches as leaders in various roles toward people of all ages coming from culturally, linguistically, economically, physically, and academically diverse places.

We can be conscious of our ontological position when listening to people's attempts to express themselves. According to Article 13 of the United Nations Convention on the Rights of the Child, "[T]he child shall have the right to freedom of expression; this right shall include freedom to seek, receive and impart information and ideas of all kinds, either orally, in writing or in print, in the form of art, or through any other media of the child's choice." Article 30 states that "in those States in which ethnic, religious or linguistic minorities or persons of indigenous origin exist, a child belonging to such a minority or who is indigenous shall not be denied the right, in community with other members of his or her group, to enjoy his or her own culture, to profess and practice his or her own religion, or to use his or her own language."

The people who are open to diversity and foster empathy, whether in schools, workplaces, or other environments, preserve these rights for Skylar, myself, and all of us through thoughtful listening, building healthy relationships, resolving conflicts, and addressing needs by embracing multiple means of expression in language and literacy. Skylar wanted to be heard from his own personal standpoint, not from the standpoint of a child with a disability. When Skylar was finally heard, his educational team was much more sensitive and responsive to his educational needs. The number of his outbursts decreased significantly as well. And I need to be heard as me—who I am—not through the lens of my deafness and speech. The primary tenet of compassionate communication is to observe and listen without evaluation, judgment, or patronization, so that the speaker can express what needs to be heard and supported.

PART 4

CONVERSATION

INTRODUCTION: DEFINING CONVERSATION

It takes two to tango.

—COMMON IDIOM

CONVERSATION INVOLVES the exchange of thoughts, ideas, and opinions among two or more people. How we converse—by taking turns to speak, making eye contact, and using personal space—is largely dependent upon social skills and etiquette, usually established within cultures. Overhearing or eavesdropping on a conversation does not always provide the full picture, because body language, subtleties, and implied context beneath the spoken words are absent from the bystander. A person can listen to an entire conversation and still be unclear about what is being discussed. Through conversations, we can chitchat, banter, tell stories, discuss ideas, share information, debate issues, and solve problems. As much as deaf or hard of hearing people desire to join in conversations, the quick volley of words, phrases, and quips renders them completely lost and isolated. Being aware of how we converse can be a benefit to everyone, regardless of their hearing ability.

TWO TRUTHS AND A LIE

PUNS AND JOKES can be amusing, because they play with reality. Puns exploit the different possible meanings of a word, and jokes contain short stories with a funny punch line. Telling ethnic jokes, however, requires one to tread carefully. Such jokes are an attempt at humor based on stereotypes, and they can go woefully wrong. Most puns evoke a mild groan, but some jokes can be hurtful or offensive. Humor surrounding deafness can go both ways, depending on which perspective it comes from—hearing or deaf.

My daughter, Kara, once had a class exercise in which she had to make three statements about herself, and one had to be false. The rest of her class had to figure out which statement was the lie by asking her questions. Her statements were as follows: I have two older brothers, I have a guinea pig named Moose, and my mom is deaf. In reality, she has only one older brother. However, her classmates and her teacher wouldn't believe that her mom was deaf. They asserted that this statement was the fib! One classmate even piped up and retorted, "My mom is deaf too! She never listens to me either!"

The humor seen in this game of two truths and a lie occurred because Kara's perspective was different than her classmates'. Her classmates couldn't believe that her mother *really* is deaf, because they'd had no exposure to the concept that mothers can be deaf. Having two older brothers and a guinea pig named Moose made more sense and appeared *normal* compared to having an *unusual* mom.

Contrary to what might be expected, hearing children in families with deaf or hard of hearing parents have perfectly intelligible and appropriate speech patterns, language usage, and social skills. We must be reminded that hearing children with a deaf parent are inevitably part of the hearing world. They all can have hearing mothers or fathers as well as hearing grandparents, aunts and uncles, neighbors, teachers, and friends and classmates in their environment. And we must distinguish between deafness (as in Kara's mother) and not listening (as in her classmate's mother) when it comes to meeting children's physical, mental, and emotional needs. Furthermore, we must distinguish between gentle happenstance humor, such as this classroom game, and ethnic jokes that are simply not funny. I've certainly been on the receiving end of distasteful jokes, some even bordering on bullying. It is surprising how people today are more aware when it comes to joking about ethnicity, race, and culture, but not so much when it comes to my deafness.

Some people think it's a joke that I don't hear at all. Some people will even announce, "Wow! You don't LOOK deaf!" Seriously, what does a deaf person *look* like? Occasionally, people will ask me, covering their lips while either increasing the volume of their voices or moving closer to me, "Can you hear me now? Can you hear me now?! Can you hear me NOW?!" Or they sneak up behind my back and shout, "Can you hear me?!" When I turn around, only because I sensed someone is right behind me, then it is declared that yes, I can hear at whatever level of loudness put forth my way. However, I explain that if one sneaks up on someone without saying anything at all, most people will naturally sense that there is someone behind them. Almost always, there is a retort: "Well, I was joking? Can't you take a joke?" I have also been a victim of "joking" that actually involved sneaking up on me at an overnight camp. *As an adult.* I don't recall ever being teased as a child at various sleep-away camps. I was a counselor for a YMCA camp in northern Michigan for three weeks, killing the time between a summer session and fall semester at college and making a little extra money to cover my tuition. One of the lifeguards discovered that she could wake me up in the middle of the night by stomping on the cabin floor. For nights on end, she would demonstrate this to an ever-growing crowd of her coworkers and even the children attending the camp. And when I asked her to stop, I received the same response: "Geez, you can't take a joke?" She eventually stopped waking me up but soon discovered that she could easily spook me on a narrow, wooded path on my way to the outhouse at any time of day or night. When I went to talk to the camp director, I was reprimanded: "Can't you take a joke? This is what camp is all about." I understood that a lot of pranks are played at camp, but still, most pranks are made between cabins, teams, or group members of the camp. A prank on a single and susceptible person is actually bullying. I felt that my deafness was singled out and taken advantage of. I can take a joke when it's good, clean camp fun, but not so well when it is directed at my vulnerability, especially at night.

Because I have absolutely no hearing, people often assume that I use American Sign Language. Some people, upon finding out that I am deaf, enthusiastically announce, "I know sign language too!" And then they proceed to demonstrate several crude and offensive gestures. Indeed, this gets really old. When I try to explain American Sign Language is not just full of pantomime and gestures, I get the same comeback: "Just joking!" But all of these "jokes" are no laughing matter; they are not even technically jokes, for there are no stories and no punch lines. Resorting to claims of joking only serves as a futile save from a faux pas.

Puns, idioms, sayings, and sarcasm are often difficult to lipread because of the unpredictability of the words and phrases being twisted around, but when they are written down, I can surely grasp the humor being conveyed. However, there are some jokes pinpointing deafness, or even any ethnicity, race, culture, or ability, that are reprehensible. I am often reluctant to welcome those who view me only through the lens of my deafness, because their perceptions—their "jokes"—are usually false, deficit-centered, or downright mean. I certainly understand that their perceptions come from their center as hearing persons. But when I'm implored to view such concepts as a joke, my inner *fight, flight, or freeze* mechanisms are quickly put in gear, and I become wary and guarded. Of course, I see my world through both the lens of my deafness and through the lens of who I am as a person. Many times, like binoculars, the lenses merge as one, and other times, they are separate. And those who listen, and listen kindly, about who I am and the ramifications of being deaf, are the ones who I am most likely to trust in my life.

Joking aside, many people live in multiple worlds and fluidly move from one to another. They can be multilingual and choose the language or dialect according to the situation they are in. One person can speak African-American English in her family and community, the jargon of her position as a firefighter, and the English spoken in her children's school. Additionally, people can be multicultural and shift what they wear, how they conduct themselves, and what traditions and rites they observe. And they joke around in appropriate situations. As a wife, mother, friend, family member, educator, author, canoeist, hiker, cross-country skier, and snowshoer, I live in a hearing world, but I also live in my own solitary deaf world. I am not part of a Deaf community. The members of this community proudly characterize themselves as Deaf (indeed with a capital D), meaning they are part of a specific group who share a language (such as American Sign Language) and a culture. They do not think of themselves as having a disability, rather they are members of a linguistic and cultural minority. Because I am not part of this community, people often ask what I have against the Deaf community. The answer is absolutely nothing.

There are many communities, cultures, and languages all around us that we are not a member of or even opposed to. Some people have asked me if members of the Deaf community might reject me as a person who actively attempts to pass as a hearing person, but so far, this has not been my experience. Interestingly, the people who have asked me this question were black males. "Passing for white" and "passing for hearing" turned out to be a shared concept that described our assimilation into the white majority. However, the members of the Deaf community who I have met over my lifetime were just as friendly to me as anyone could be in any interlingual and intercultural situation.

Furthermore, we must recognize that although there are Deaf community members living among us, there are others who define their deafness simply as the inability to hear well enough to rely on their ears as a way of obtaining information. Still others consider themselves to be hard of hearing, meaning that they have a hearing loss but use speech and lipreading as their usual form of communication. And of course, there are some, like good ole' grandpa, who don't hear very well but will totally deny it.

In my unique case, I have to constantly explain that yes, I am totally deaf, but no, I do not know American Sign Language. And no, I did not go to Gallaudet University, a higher-education institution with programs specifically designed to accommodate signing deaf and hard of hearing students. Then I have to explain again, that yes, I can speak, lipread, and even read and write, but no, I really don't hear at all. Now that cochlear implants, jokingly called "bionic ears," are becoming more well known and are touted as a "cure" for hearing loss (they aren't), I have to explain that I am not interested in having a medically invasive procedure and enduring intensive rehabilitation in order to train my brain to accept and adjust to the sounds electronically inputted through the implant. And when I do not offer such explanations of who I am, either from lack of chance or by choice, some people become uncomfortable or prone to making objectionable jokes.

In total fairness, there are classic jokes deaf people tell to poke fun at hearing people. One even appeared in a 2008 Super Bowl commercial for Pepsi. In the sixty-second ad played out silently, two deaf guys are driving to their friend Bob's house to watch the football game, but they can't remember the address. All of the houses on the street are dark, so one of the guys solves the problem by laying on the car horn. One by one, the lights in all the houses come on, except for one, and that's how the two guys know where Bob lives. This is a kind of humor that people who are deaf or hard of hearing can appreciate.

I, too, have a sense of humor, and I sometimes make fun of the idiocy of some hearing people. One of my favorites is about my ability to drive a car. One day that had been particularly too long for me, I was anxious to get home, because snow was beginning to fall and I was feeling the sniffles coming on. I climbed into my Subaru Outback and started for home. Thinking about supper that night, I decided I could manage a slight detour to the local grocery store, which I knew wouldn't be crowded, because folks in Michigan are not ones to clear the shelves of bread and milk at the slightest hint of a blizzard.

After winding through the aisles, picking up items for making chicken soup for my head cold, I looked for the check-out clerk, who knew I was deaf. I didn't have the patience to deal with the tangle of questions, always coming in seemly random order, as I unloaded my groceries onto the belt: "Did you find everything you need? Paper or plastic? Do you have a Rewards Card? Credit or Cash? How are the roads out there?" Alas, it seemed that the familiar clerk was not there that day. My nerves were beginning to wear thin in direct proportion to the amount of accumulating snow outside. I muddled through the confusion of the check-out lanes and started off with my cart, first checking behind me to make sure that I didn't miss hearing any last-minute instruction or forget something. And I made sure I didn't have any un-paid-for items that might set off the theft alarms, something that did happen to me once.

The snow was accumulating enough to cause the wheels of the cart to coat with ice and stick in opposite directions. I jostled the cart abruptly back and forth several times to shake off the snow and ice, as I made my way through the parking lot. Finally, I reached my Outback, found my snowbrush in the backseat, and brushed the snow off the back hatch. I pulled and pulled on the latch to crack the built-up ice and opened the hatch to unload my groceries. It was then that the familiar check-out clerk, who was actually outside collecting shopping carts in advance of the storm, spotted me in surprise and asked, "Is that your car? I didn't know that you can drive." She said that she had always assumed that I had taken a cab or had a relative drive me to the store and back home. Being used to this kind of question, I normally kindly explain to people that deaf and hard of hearing people are fully capable of driving. However, at this particular time, I was at the tail end of a long day, wasn't feeling well, wanted to finish my snowy commute, and was quite annoyed. At the same time, I noticed my roof rack, which extends well beyond the sides of the car, so that my husband, Klaus, and I can carry several canoes and kayaks at once, and upon which many people have bumped their heads on in parking lots. So, Klaus slit four bright yellow tennis balls and slipped one on each end of the rack. If someone doesn't see them, at least the tennis balls make for a softer bump than the iron rod. Trying not to roll my eyes and groan in response to the question, and, with great exasperation, I simply blurted out, "That's why I have those tennis balls on the ends of the rack. . . it makes me more visible!" Unbelievably, the clerk did not catch the sarcasm. She actually thought it was an awesome idea and said she would pass that information on to other people, like her grandfather and her uncle who don't hear very well! Although seeing an oversized roof rack capped with bright yellow tennis balls is common among canoeists and kayakers, the store clerk was on her way to start a trend among deaf and hard of hearing people! I know that it wasn't very nice of me but, seriously, the joke was on her.

SKIPPING STONES

FAMILIES OR A GROUP of friends, of all ages, at a summer cottage are invariably drawn to skipping stones, particularly in the evening, as the sun goes down and the lake in front of them is calm. There is always bantering, teasing, and whoops—conversations that I don't hear—as everyone throws their stone and tries to get it to bounce on the flat surface as many times as they can before the stone sinks into the water. Katarina, a studious fourth-grader with a great sense of humor, who spoke both English and Russian fluently, landed on my special education caseload for writing, specifically for spelling. I felt that Katarina, as a bilingual child, was most likely not disabled; she was just beginning to learn how English words are spelled. Too often, culturally and linguistically diverse children like Katarina are placed in special or remedial education and taught in a disabling context. No matter, she and I were both having a wonderful time exploring the similarities and differences of English and Russian letters and sounds.

Whenever I am supporting children in their exploration of written expression skills, I always start with the children's interests. Katarina was fascinated with wild animals, particularly reptiles, such as crocodiles, alligators, snakes, lizards, and turtles. She also loved amphibians, such as frogs, toads, and salamanders. In a happenstance conversation with her about skipping stones over water, our young herpetologist pointed out to me that many people also call the activity *little frogs* or *sending the frogs out*. She squealed with delight at anything related to herpetology and often used this subject for her free writing assignments.

Even though Katarina had no difficulties thinking of what to write about, spelling was her nemesis. In beginning a research project about poisonous animals in the forest, she wrote, "My projit is obot difrint posinis anamals en the forst." A major feature of the Russian sound system is the absence of the short-long vowel differentiation as well as the lack of *diphthongs*, the sound formed by the combination of two vowels in a single syllable (like in *pie* and *coin*). Katarina needed to learn that vowels in English are vexingly arbitrary, and even one vowel can have many variations of its sound. So, I pulled out a chart of English vowels for her to keep track of; for example, a long /u/ sound can be composed of the letters *oo (room)*, *ew (grew)*, or *ue (blue)*.

Because Katarina was smitten with the ins and outs of her two languages, she asked if she could invite four of her friends to our weekly sessions. Katarina knew that I don't hear, but she also knew that the two of us got along just fine regardless. However, I explained that as much as I would love to have her invite her friends, a larger group is much harder for me to keep up. Not only that, it was against the school rules for me to work with her friends, who were not on my caseload. But Katarina, with hands pressed together, persisted and pleaded: "Please! Please! Please! Some of my friends speak Russian and English, and some of them speak just English. When I'm with my Russian friends, we all speak Russian. But if there is only ONE person who does not know Russian, we all speak English. I promise we'll speak English! I promise!"

I was impressed with her explanation of how they would be sure to include me. Of course, Katarina is not deaf and wouldn't understand that it is next to impossible for deaf people to keep up with the volley of conversations between friends, regardless of what language they speak. Ultimately, I couldn't resist her pleas, so after getting permission from the principal and all the parents involved, we set up a time outside of Katarina's regularly scheduled sessions for me to meet her friends to share their written pieces and explore spelling differences in English and Russian. Because school was almost out for the summer, I decided to put together several writing prompts surrounding summertime fun, such as camp programs, swimming, and even skipping stones. Even so, I was still a bit nervous as the day approached. How was I going to manage a bunch of fourth graders I didn't know and two different languages?

Much to my delight, Katarina took charge. She introduced her friends, writing their names down on my office whiteboard. She explained to her friends that they must face me when speaking to me and talk in English. They also needed to take turns talking. Ultimately, they all conversed with each other and me diligently, speaking one at a time, without impatience or patronization. And each one of these children made sure that I, and the others, all understood. These children were in fourth grade! My inner voice filled with longing; I so much desired more inclusion among groups of people like Katarina and her friends.

Connecting with people, networking, and making new friends can be fraught with a range of emotions, from anxiety, inadequacy, inferiority, humiliation, to embarrassment. This is true at times for anyone, but for deaf or hard of hearing people among hearing people, there is the added stress of simply not being able to hear. It doesn't matter if the deaf person is innately friendly and outgoing or naturally reserved and shy. Being within a group of hearing people, fully aware of their mouth movements, laughter, and frowns, but not keeping up with the fast-moving volley of language, chatter, and conversations can give a deaf person a huge sense of aloneness and loneliness along with a feeling of being ungrounded and out of control. Occasionally, out of this fog, a long-time friend or family member will notice me and tell me in brief terms what is being discussed, but the conversation speeds forward, and soon both that person and I am unable to keep up. When I step in on my own—in an attempt to be part of a conversation—I am too often politely eased out. Most of the time, people tell me what they are talking about in one or two words, but I still don't have any context or connection. Sometimes, a response will be simply: *"Oh, we're not talking about anything important."* Other times, if I insist on being part of the conversation, I am asked, *"Why is it always about you?"* Alas, it has to be about me first, only in the sense that my communication needs have to be met, before it can be about others.

Joining a conversation, particularly with those who do not know me well, is always a matter of luck as to whether I'm successful or inappropriate. I am occasionally told, *"It is rude to interrupt,"* or *"this doesn't involve you."* I can usually see that a conversation is private when people whisper into each other's ears or move away furtively. Then I know that it's none of my business. In most situations, however, all of the hearing people within earshot are part of it, gathered at the dinner table, sitting together in living rooms, and standing in groups. Why not me? Additionally, I come across people I cannot lipread at all, due to accents or moustaches, and I need someone else to repeat what was said to me. But then again, the banter rolls on while the person is telling me what was said, and soon that person needs to catch up. Many times, there is awkwardness in that people try to squirm away from me, find someone else to talk to, or just smile or nod their heads at me without even trying to make the conversation work.

When summertime came and I was still basking in the kindness of Katarina and her friends, I went out on a lake with three acquaintances, each one of us in our own solo canoe. Now, three is an awkward number. A larger group allows for more potential opportunities for one-on-one interactions without the person I'm conversing with missing out on a group conversation. On the one hand, larger groups often break up into smaller groups, and I can usually find someone to have a side conversation with on a one-to-one basis. On the other hand, too large of a group just makes for too much noise and confusion. But three or four, or even five, people carry on a conversation together of which I usually cannot follow.

While the four of us were canoeing, I could see a lot of gabbing and laughter, but I was on the outside, having absolutely no idea what they were sharing over the two hours we were together. At one point, a person pointed at a Great Blue Heron just flushed out from the bank of a channel. I could see that a conversation ensued about the heron. I made a quizzical look toward one person, who then remarked, "We're looking at the heron." I wanted to know more about what these people were saying about the heron, but knew that I would disrupt the flow of the conversation by asking questions. I knew a lot about herons as a species. I was very familiar with their physical descriptions, habitats, and behaviors from both reading and many years of observation from my canoe. But I didn't know what to ask other than general question: "What are you all saying about that heron?" And I didn't know when or how to ask without being intrusive. I paddled on, wondering if they were talking about the bird band on the heron's long leg, if they had ever seen a heron stalk and catch a fish, or that a mutual friend of ours had painted a beautiful mural of a wetland with a heron in it. I wondered what they could possibly be talking about *about* the heron.

No one wants to repeat a conversation. A closer friend is usually willing to explain to me what was said, but by then, my contribution to the conversation is moot. It's never practical to point out to my acquaintances that if each one talked to *me*, or at least made sure to face me, the others would still hear. This practice will last for maybe a minute or two, but then the conversation goes right back to normal without me. The group quickly moves on to other topics, and the whole afternoon on the lake has me one step behind, catching just fragments of conversations— and never belonging.

Returning to the cottage we were staying at and sitting down at a long table on the porch for dinner, I was still lost. Again, I can always see conversation flying around me. I am lucky if I have a person next to me willing to chat with just me, but most of the time, a dinner table has six or eight people conversing together. I never want to exclude my neighbor from the group. I'm always told about the big things—a marriage proposal, a serious accident, or the newest member of a family. Big things only come around once in a while. It's the little things. The littlest things that bring delight and comfort and enrich our lives. A sense of belonging—a sense of connection—comes from a brother looking up an interesting word in the dictionary and sharing the definition, friends sharing an uproarious laugh over an embarrassing moment from long ago, aunts describing a journey overseas, and late-night discussions on solving the world's problems.

I found some relief and company with my friends when we headed down to the beach to skip stones. On the walk down, I chatted with one friend. On the beach, I chatted with another. As we were tossing round, flat stones across the lake, I noticed that a friend suddenly turned around and smiled at someone. I looked behind me and noticed that another cottage guest, a stranger to me, must have shouted something. Perhaps an admiration for the number of skips my friend made. Perhaps they knew each other. Or perhaps that the guest was pointing out another heron across the lake. I threw more stones out, wondering what that guest said to my friend, but it didn't matter to me too much. Much more meaningful for me is what my own family and friends, and the new friends I want to get to know, are sharing. I never expect to "hear" the same amount of conversation that hearing people do, but always, my hope is to at least listen to something or two of substance in my interactions with other people—more than just seeing the heron and congratulatory shouts over skipped stones.

When I'm home at the end of the workday or over the weekend, I often deal with a huge sense of aloneness and frustration, even to the point of anger and tears for a while. I accept that I am deaf, and I realize that conversations with me can be cumbersome, disruptive, intrusive, and fragmented. I have yet to figure out how to make this work for all of us. I am often asked why I can't simply enjoy "being there." After all, hearing people do not hear *everything*. I do enjoy being there, but only to a point, at least until the sense of isolation and seeing the connections among people right in front of me, as if I was in a bubble, become too much for me to bear. However, if I counter with "What is the purpose of being with friends and family? How would it feel if everyone gathered and no one spoke at all?" I am prone to the comeback: "Are you wallowing in pity?" I'm simply not hearing. I want to be part of conversations, but there is no way I can do it alone without other people who are willing to overcome the communication barriers along with me.

Most hearing people take conversations for granted, without realizing the amount of volleying and bantering that goes on. Even the most adept lipreaders struggle to follow conversations that are dynamic, spirited, and lively. One discussion can lead to another and another. People can change their train of thought and move on to different topics quickly. Individuals can suddenly switch from a conversation with me to another conversation nearby. Hearing one another can affirm presence and a sense of belonging, but compassionate listening and reaching out from all sides of a conversation can show a deeper sense of caring, connection, and love, especially for those who don't hear.

EYES IN THE BACK OF MY HEAD

BEING AROUND a person who has turned a deaf ear, by ignoring or refusing to respond to a request, or has turned a blind eye by pretending not to notice, can be exasperating or infuriating for some people. A deaf person can certainly turn a deaf ear or a blind eye on purpose at times, but in many situations, that person is really deaf. An inquisitive third-grade child, whose name I never knew, came up to me one day in a hallway, tapped my arm, and asked if I was blind. I work in multiple buildings, so most children and staff politely acknowledge my presence, say hello, and move on. In most cases, they do not even know that I am deaf, so it was unusual for me to have a child try to strike up a conversation with me. Thinking that she was mixing up her terminology, I kindly explained that I am deaf and do not hear. But because I can see very well, I am not blind at all.

I forgot about this encounter until two days later, when yet another child asked me the same question. I also noticed that week that many children I passed in the school hallways were gawking at me as if I was famous or something. Usually if someone is giving me a quizzical look, I look around behind me to see what I've missed hearing, or I might ask if the person was talking to me or not. Because this was a hallway full of children, I started to wonder what was going on. Finally, at the end of the week, a classroom teacher came up to me and announced that all of the third- and fourth-grade classes in the school had been reading and learning about Helen Keller. She remarked what a perfect example I was for their discussions: "a modern-day Helen Keller!" So, that's where all the questions and stares were coming from!

When I shared this story with the principal, she threw her head back and laughed. Then she suddenly stopped and reflected: "Wait! That's not right!" Although it does make for an amusing story, the reality is that we shouldn't be conflating disabilities. I am deaf, but not blind. I certainly don't read in braille. I don't even know fingerspelling in the hand, a communication method that Anne Sullivan taught Helen Keller.

94

The principal and I were certainly not condemning reading lessons or discussions about people such as Helen Keller. Of course, Helen Keller, born in 1880, was extraordinary in her time, and children should learn about her challenges and accomplishments. However, being deaf is not the same as being deaf-blind, as she was. Instead of telling the students that I was a modern-day Helen Keller, the teacher could have asked the children to speculate what the world would be like if all people were deaf and blind. How would we communicate? How would we function as a society? And how would seeing and hearing people fit into this deaf and blind world?

It was not long before Jeremy, a fifth-grader who was tall for his age and a presence to match, abruptly stopped right in front of me in the hallway. We were almost nose-to-nose. He had heard about my deafness through the school grapevine. "Watch this!" Jeremy announced, as he gathered his friends and classmates around to see. Jeremy moved his lips in a wildly exaggerated manner: "Hellllooo!" As soon as I responded with a hello back, all those watching laughed uproariously and dashed off. It became apparent to me that Jeremy was proudly showing off how I could understand what he was saying without using his voice. I reminded Jeremy that yes, I do not hear and that I lipread, but that it was also not nice to make fun of a person with a disability or difference. But Jeremy persisted, and other children in his class were starting the game too.

After too many days of this game, I was starting to feel like a side-show freak. After I had a dream one night that Jeremy was actually profiting at my expense, I realized that it was a high time for this stunt to stop. Instead of resorting to punitive discipline, I decided to try a restorative justice approach, in which I gathered the children in Jeremy's class for a short council on diversity, so we could talk through this situation. I called up six volunteers, one by one. Jeremy eagerly volunteered as well. I lined them up in front of the whiteboard, looked at each child, and wrote a characteristic above each child's head: Jeremy was *tall*, Addison was a *girl*, Jayden had *brown skin*, Albert had a *birthmark*, Ava was the *youngest*, and Luciana spoke *Spanish*. And I wrote *deaf* in my space on the board.

I asked for a volunteer to say hello to Jeremy, Addison, Jayden, Albert, Ava, Luciana, and me. That volunteer eagerly came up and said hello to each one of us in a kind and appropriate manner. A few children even put their hands out for a shake. Smiles were made all around. When I asked for a volunteer to come up and say hello in a teasingly and exaggerated manner, no one was willing. I explained that the lesson was not only about diversity, but also about *pragmatic language*, which involves social interactions with others—the what, when, and how we say things, our body language, eye contact, introducing and staying on topic, and its appropriateness in a given situation. If it is not appropriate to say hello in an offensive manner to someone who is tall, is a girl, has brown skin or a birthmark, is the youngest, and speaks Spanish, then it is certainly not appropriate toward me or any other person with a disability or difference either.

Admittedly, not many people are deaf. And not many people are blind. Fewer are both deaf and blind. And even among deaf, blind, or deaf-blind people, there is a wide range of severities and implications of hearing losses and vision impairments. Furthermore, many people, including deaf and hard of hearing people, have what is considered an *invisible disability*, a disability or chronic illness that is not outwardly or immediately apparent to an onlooker. Because the impairments or symptoms are invisible, an invisible disability can lead to misunderstandings, false perceptions and judgments, and unreasonably high expectations as compared to someone who has a *visible disability*, such as a person in a wheelchair (who, by contrast, may encounter much lower expectations than their actual capabilities).

I once had a meeting with a deaf parent at a different school. Seeing that this parent was using American Sign Language, one of my colleagues asked if she was the interpreter for the meeting. I introduced her as the parent and said we were actually waiting for the interpreter to arrive before starting the meeting. My colleague responded with an apology of misunderstanding that the parent "doesn't look like a real deaf person." My exasperated inner voice shouted, "Seriously, what does a REAL deaf person look like?" Of course, many hearing people who encounter someone who is deaf or hard of hearing find the concept quite a novelty. Teachers used me as a representation of Helen Keller, and Jeremy put my lipreading skills on display to his friends.

Because deafness and hearing losses are invisible and uncommon, I have, on occasions, found myself in confrontational or even hazardous situations only because I have unintentionally turned a deaf ear to someone. Despite being deaf, I have done many things alone. I love to go out solo in my canoe. I love to hike. I especially love to cross-country ski. Of course, I do these things as safely as I can, always letting someone know where I am and when I am expected to be back.

But venturing into our local grocery store sometimes proves to be more dangerous than being on the lakes or out in the woods. My husband, Klaus, asked me to add kitty litter to my grocery list, which was curious because we have never had cats. It turned out that Klaus spilled motor oil in the barn and needed to spread kitty litter to absorb it. He asked me to buy kitty litter that was cheap and mostly made of clay.

When I arrived in the aisle that contained the pet supplies, I was awed and dismayed at the wide variety of kitty litter. There was an array of scoopable, clumping, crystal, flushable, natural, odor-sealing, scented, premium, double-duty, extra-strength, triple-action, and even multi-cat litter from the top to the bottom of the shelves. I stood in the middle of the aisle scratching my head. I studied each brand, looking at prices and reading the content of clay. Suddenly, a woman behind me angrily rammed her cart into the back of my heels, because I was so focused that I didn't move out of the way. Startled, I turned around, stepped aside, and explained that I didn't hear her. I didn't mean to be rude. She went on to admonish me that because I was deaf, I shouldn't be shopping alone in the first place. In a frenzy, she went to find the manager to report a "poor deaf person lost in the store." She brought the manager back to show him that I was deaf without a companion and that I needed help. The manager, a friendly man who knew me as a familiar shopper, smiled and asked if I needed help. "Sure," I responded, "would you help me find kitty litter that is cheap and made of clay for my husband to clean up spilt motor oil, please?" And I thanked the woman for finding the manager for me. She sneered and wasn't convinced that I was quite capable of surviving a trek through a grocery store. It was quite eerie as she followed and kept an eye on me while I finished my shopping trip, unloaded my groceries into my car, and drove off.

Although incidents like this don't stop me from going to grocery stores and other places on my own, my guard is always heightened in busy places. I am not afraid of snakes or bears in the wild, but am much more nervous among the hustle and bustle of strangers. I don't *need* a companion, but it is more comfortable to have a sense of safety in numbers among close friends and family. I have been physically buffaloed. I've tripped over things while walking and even cut my finger with a knife while cooking, when people have demanded me to lipread them. I was twice chased down and grabbed in a parking lot when one of my purchased items accidentally set off the theft alarm. And I was angrily yelled at, with a gesture of choking my neck: "You! You! You need eyes in the back of your head!" Most often, I am simply told to stop being so rude or to get out of the way.

I am reluctant to admit to feeling weary and battered, because then I am susceptible to admonishments on how to handle such situations. I am confronted with the dynamic of blaming-the-victim, in that I am responsible for the perpetrator's frustration and aggression toward me. Perhaps I should hire a companion. Perhaps I should wear a T-shirt indicating that I am deaf. Perhaps I should carry an explanatory card to hand out to everyone around me. And perhaps I should drive the electric cart (with bright yellow tennis balls?) to make my deafness more visible. However, such suggestions can actually make me more vulnerable. A companion could make decisions for me without checking with me first. My T-shirt could bring on stares or mocking. Handing out cards could frustrate people, in that they would have to stop and read it. And I could be scolded for driving an electric cart without an apparent physical disability. If I mention an incident involving someone known to a mutual friend, there is often a defense: "He didn't understand you," or "She was just kidding around," or even "That's not possible, he is a very nice person." However, I am a fine mesh filter for separating the "nice" people. The nice people are the ones who admit their ignorance, reach out, and offer to repair the situation. Otherwise, there is no good way out of dealing with rebukes, finger-wagging, reprimands, and even at times, physical hostility when the blame for my inability to hear is squarely on me.

Defining rudeness is dependent upon cultural and civil mores. Language, customs, values, and behaviors accepted as appropriate or inappropriate varies by cultures or population groups. We all err at times, especially in intercultural communication, whether we hear or not. Therefore, there is no need to adhere to rigidity; letting go of minor slights is necessary for building relationships and peaceful coexistence. Communication and conversation calls for gentleness and commitment from all parties involved. A person with a communication disability, such as a hearing loss or a speech and language disorder (e.g., stuttering), shouldn't be allowed to get away with blatantly rude behavior, but persons with normal hearing must realize that they need to exercise patience and flexibility to deal with differences in social rules of discourse. No matter, a basic sense of what is right versus what is wrong is universal in *all* cultures. No one should be standing nose-to-nose and mocking, ramming shopping carts into the back of heels, buffaloing, or even gesturing a choke around a neck to anyone else. In fact, these actions border as outward threats or assaults.

Surely, eyes in the back of my head would be helpful; better yet, being able to hear in a hearing world. However, I cannot change my physical characteristics. I can only explain that I don't mean to be rude. And I can try to foster a stronger sense of advocacy and empowerment, not just for those with disabilities, but also toward creating a kinder environment that is inclusive for all of us. When Jeremy and his classmates learned about diversity, pragmatic language, and kindness, word got around among their parents, many of whom personally thanked me for sharing my experience. This was an authentic lesson that impressed the children—and the adults—more than categorizing me with Helen Keller.

PART 5

READING

INTRODUCTION: DEFINING READING

Now I know my ABCs.

—"ALPHABET SONG"

READING IS DEFINED in different ways, depending on the underlying theories of reading processes and comprehension. Our knowledge of how people learn to read, and the process of reading itself, has expanded over the years, becoming increasingly multidisciplinary with contributions from fields, such as sociology, anthropology, linguistics, psychology, and neurology. Most researchers agree that reading is an intricate and intimate interaction between the reader, the text, and the author in order to create meaning and foster reflection. The reader sets a purpose for reading, employs background knowledge and experiences, and decodes letters and words to make sense of the material. Comprehension can be literal, interpretative, or critical. Texts are offered in a multitude of genres and forms, and they range in complexity. Authors bring their own style, tone, and mood to convey their messages.

Reading is a learned and practiced skill; it is not "instinctive." Despite the stereotype that deaf and hard of hearing people are unable to read past a third- or fourth-grade level, many are proficient and fluent readers. The belief that reading requires the ability to decode the sounds of letters (phonological coding) has distracted educators from the possibility that there are other pathways for deaf children who are learning to read. This same belief system impacts hearing children with learning disabilities or who otherwise struggle to learn to read. Teachers who focus solely on decoding prevent these children from taking advantage of other strategies, such as using background knowledge and experiences, vocabulary, language processing, emotion and motivation, and connections, or even overlooking that students may need glasses. Even though reading seems automatic for most of us, it must be recognized as a complex process that requires continuous practice before it is proficient, fluent, and gratifying.

THE POETRY SLAM

READING PROVIDES information, understanding, pleasure, and new concepts and ideas; it lets us travel, dream, and even escape from the realities of the world. But not everyone likes to read. For some, reading can be an arduous process. People of all ages who struggle with literacy begin to devise coping strategies for hiding this fact from others and avoiding the dreaded task of decoding and making meaning of words and phrases.

Sam was a fifth-grader who claimed he was averse to reading. He would feign all kinds of allergic reactions when near books. He said they were dusty. They were moldy too. His eyes itched. His nose would run. His ears would plug up, and he could not hear. His tongue would swell up. He would show me every single little bump on his arms and hands and insist that I let him visit the school nurse or, at least, hand over the box of tissues. At the same time, Sam had a classmate, William, who implored him to "stop acting like a baby." William wasn't keen on reading either, but he would pick up a book—any book—and go off in the corner and pretend to read. Sam noticed that one of the books William picked up had little ponies, kittens, and rainbows all over the cover and without mercy, teased William about reading "girl books."

Sam and William were in the same after-school football league, and although they both were good at math, they detested reading. Reading was not an automatic process for them, and most of the books and other reading materials available in the school didn't even spark their interest. I promised both of them that I would teach them how to read better, but the rule was that they must find their own material and bring it to my office each day. It didn't matter what genre, format, or level the materials was. Anything that they wanted to read was welcomed. Sam brought in a newspaper article about a tornado that had destroyed houses in a neighboring town, and William brought in his older brother's driver's education book. We discussed the purposes for reading these materials. Sam remarked he was really scared when the tornado warning sirens went off when he was babysitting his younger siblings. He knew that going down to the basement was a safety measure, but he wanted to know more details about this particular tornado, because he saw in the newspaper that houses were flattened or completely blown away. William mentioned that his brother didn't know that he had swiped the driver's education book, but he promised he would put it back where he found it. He wanted to learn how to read it ahead of time, because in a few years, he, too, could learn how to drive. He didn't want to lose his chance by not learning how to read by then.

Over time and through a variety of self-chosen materials, I taught the boys strategies for reading. I showed them how the language used to describe tornadoes and driving could help them decode words. I showed them what to do when they got stuck on words they struggled to decode or didn't know the meaning of. I reminded them that reading is all about making sense, not just reading letters and words. And I assured them that they didn't have to be perfect word-by-word readers. They could read ahead a little bit and go back to figure out unknown words or to double-check their comprehension. If they didn't know the meaning of a word, they could still read ahead and see if they could figure out the meaning by using context. I also told them that they could decipher multisyllabic ("long") words by saying the first few letters and mumbling the rest. Because I asserted that people get better with practice, just like they were both doing in football, I would give them twenty minutes per day to read silently and independently.

By having the boys choose their materials and through learning a set of reading strategies, we were well on our way to having engaging and productive reading sessions. It was not long before I was able to introduce some chapters from quality books of high interest to boys, (such as those by Dan Gutman, Gary Paulsen, and Louis Sachar), as well as sections from science and social studies textbooks. Sam, no longer allergic to books, went on to try writing his own rap and poetry throughout his middle school years. In high school, one of his proudest moments was winning a local poetry slam sponsored by a teen center. And William became more confident that he would be able to pass his driver's test when the time came. He even began thinking beyond learning to drive and to becoming an engineer for one of our auto industries.

We ask the perennial question if our identities—who we are and what matters to us—are what we create ourselves, or if they are created by other people around us. Likewise, we can ask whether literacy is something we create as part of our identity, or if it is created for us. Too often, boys, particularly boys of color, are victims of the political tension surrounding who gets to be literate and who does not. For boys like Sam and William, literacy is regarded as a possession—usually owned by the schools and the dominant society—that ignores their languages, literacies, race, and masculinity. And too often, literacy is defined for those who are deaf. They are not expected to learn to read well, a mind-set that has continued to persist.

My identity as an author is even prone to speculation. Friends, colleagues, and family who know me well have suggested that I write a memoir about my educational experience and learning to read and write. Most of them think my academic book, *Reading Upside Down,* is about being deaf and are surprised to learn that it is not. And people who don't know me, and who pick up the book, are surprised to find out that I'm deaf. My deafness is mentioned briefly in just a few paragraphs in the preface, but it still does not answer the specific question of how I learned to read and write.

Reading and writing—strengthening and deepening language and literacy—are processes that one endeavors to learn over a lifetime; they are not simply accomplished at the end of first grade, third grade, or upon high school graduation. At the same time, it is ironic that deaf and hard of hearing people are not expected to read or write well or at all, even though reading and writing, especially with the use of technology (captioning, texting, email, and websites), is a particularly viable means of communication and access to educational and economic success. Viewing people through a deficit lens leads to erroneous assumptions about their ability to learn language and literacy and unwittingly creates a vicious cycle of opportunity gaps, which in turn, creates achievement gaps in our schools and employment gaps in our workplaces.

I was nearly three years old when my parents discovered I was deaf; shortly after that, they found a quality intervention program. With a goal toward fostering literacy development, every item in my small classroom was clearly labeled. These words were neatly written on durable cardstock of approximately four by eight inches in size. The door had the word *door* taped on it. Several chairs had the word *chair* hung from them. Even the drinking fountain had the word *water* posted on the wall above it. Posters containing pictures of things had smaller labels, too, such as *cat, house, toothbrush,* and so forth. There were a lot of picture books, often with themes, such as farm animals. Each page contained one item with the associated word under it. So even though I couldn't hear or say the words, I surely learned what they looked like in print!

Just like at any typical preschool, we had story hour twice a day, first thing in the morning and right before going home on the school bus. I remember thoroughly enjoying story time and always jostled for the best spot on the carpet. However, the teachers were conscious of making sure they were facing our small group of children as they read aloud. Being mindful that this group of children had varying levels of hearing losses, they spoke clearly and pointed to words and pictures where appropriate. They provided ample time for clarification and discussion. They even reread some of our favorite stories several times to assure deeper understanding. And they left the books out on the shelves for us to try to read, or "pretend read," on our own. From preschool on, I grew up surrounded by educators who had absolutely no doubt that I *could,* and *would,* learn to read and write. The concept of *mainstreaming,* the practice of educating children with disabilities for specific time periods in regular classrooms, was still in its experimental stages. This was long before laws were enacted to protect my rights to an education.

Eventually, I repeated second grade in a fully inclusive classroom in my neighborhood school, and I attended public schools and colleges for the remainder of my educational career. Interestingly, the practice of *inclusion,* an approach in which a child with a disability spends all of his or her time in general education, was not conceived of back then, but it was indeed the experience I had. Mainstreaming focuses on placing children with special needs in general education classrooms for portions of the day, depending on their ability to succeed socially and academically. Inclusion makes no distinction between special and general education—the focus being on the children, not their disabilities; all children in inclusive classrooms are accepted, respected, and taught regardless of their abilities. Although my teachers objectively acknowledged and accommodated my deafness, they still maintained the same curricular expectations for me as for the rest of my classmates.

I had no qualms about being one of the first, and to my knowledge, the only child with a disability at this school. I didn't care if I had to repeat second grade in order to ensure my academic success. My classmates were the childhood friends that I played kick-the-can with, went swimming with in the club pool, and rode bikes with around the block. Instead of leaving alone on a school bus for my special school, I started walking to school with my neighbors. We picked up more and more children as we got closer to the school, creating a little crowd by the time we got there. On the way home, I finally got to take my turn to ride in the back of the mail carrier's Jeep, literally on top of the pile of bundled mail and packages. Joe, our gregarious and generous mail carrier, even asked me when my birthday was. So, I started getting a birthday card every year from him, just like every other delighted child in the neighborhood. Talk about inclusion! I became a part of the school and the community—one who was learning language and literacy as much as I could along the way.

I was fortunate to start out reading very young, even before learning to speak. And I learned to read without being tested and measured on every inch of my progress, especially during the time it took me to "catch up" with my peers. Sam and William, on the other hand, started out in kindergarten with parents expecting them to learn to read at school. Both sets of parents reported that they knew it was important to read aloud to their children and did so on occasion, but they insisted that the teaching of reading, writing, and math was to happen at school. To them, it was the school's job to teach and their job to be parents. Alas, Sam and William were "behind" right from the beginning and never caught up. Throughout their elementary years, they took standardized tests on a regular basis that kept noting their achievement as below target. Finally, Sam was given a diagnosis of "emotional impairment" and William a diagnosis of "language impairment," And both were placed in special education. How ironic. I had a medically identified disability, but grew up in an accepting and inclusive environment. Sam and William, however, were placed in special education for dubious reasons and were covertly segregated into resource rooms. Then they were assigned words on flash cards, phonics lessons in an isolated and sequential manner, worksheets, and bland low-level books, all of which further disengaged them.

Unfortunately, the days of overt segregation prior to the Civil Rights Act of 1964 and Education for All Handicapped Children Act of 1975 have given way to covert segregation in special education and resource rooms today. The pattern of within-school segregation based on achievement or perceived ability has persisted for decades without much public outcry, even though millions of students, teachers, and administrators observe it at school every day, and it has been well documented by education researchers. I was fortunate to attend a school with a progressive and inclusive belief system, regardless of laws that existed to exclude me as *uneducable*. I was lucky that my formative years of learning to read were sandwiched between these years of overt and covert segregation and long before the years of intense standardized testing.

Literacy is a deeply personal and lifelong endeavor. And literacy and education are by far not interchangeable; one certainly can be literate without a diploma or a degree. Simply defined, *literacy* means the ability to read and write; but it is far more than that. After all, there are many kinds of literacy: academic, adult, basic, functional, computer, cultural, economic, emergent, family, media, and workplace. Literacy is also seen on a continuum in which one can be highly literate, low literate, or even illiterate in any of the forms of literacies. My academic literacy is at a level where I can do research and write papers for professional journals, but my computer or economic literacy is not something to reckon with. After all, an illiterate person is someone who cannot access (or produce) texts that are seen as significant within a given situation. That same person, in another situation, may be quite literate. When I brought my husband's automobile repair manual to share with a reluctant fourth-grade reader, he thought that my husband must have been stupid to need a manual to fix our car. He said that he and his dad could fix cars without even looking at a book. On the other hand, a German grandmother with limited English, unable to read the electric bill or *The New York Times,* may be able to read aloud children's books to her grandchildren with proficiency and delightful animation.

When a number of cultures coexist within the same society, it is more likely that we will encounter various concepts of what constitutes being literate. Instead of discussing literacy as denoting only one form, a more accurate and inclusive way to describe practices that surround language and print is to use the term *literacies*. There is no one form of literacy that is legitimate or at the right level. Furthermore, children like Sam, William, and myself when I was young, in particular, have a wide developmental range of reading and writing skills. We were rooted in languages and literacies that we started our young lives with, and then we learned the languages and literacies of school. In fact, policy makers and corporations that design tests are basically defining literacy from their own ethnocentric position. In other words, affluent children have an advantage, because their background is similar to that of the test makers, so they are comfortable with the vocabulary and subtle sub-cultural assumptions of the tests. I have seen urban children struggle with standardized test items about boarding horses, traveling to one of NASA's space centers, or catching chicken pox. Literacy defined by policy makers, testing corporations, and even employers may not entirely match with a person's background knowledge, language, or literacies, but it doesn't mean that person is underachieving, incompetent, or incapable. Certainly, we should teach reading as a basic skill, but we must also acknowledge culture, first languages, background knowledge, and motivation as part of the instruction in reading and writing. When we embrace and empower an expanded view of literacies, then we can see how opportunities abound for learning and strengthening language, culture, identity, and literacies for all people of all ages.

OH, GEE

WE MUST get back to the basics! So goes the rallying cry of those who think education policy is becoming too convoluted these days, especially with regard to diversity and literacy instruction. When parents or school administrators assert, sometimes quite vocally or even through school board members, lawyers, and politicians, that *the basics* mean teaching the nuts and bolts of phonics, my inner voice always groans, "Oh, gee."

Daniel, a ninth-grader, was a slow letter-by-letter and word-by-word reader, who was identified in special education as dyslexic. He had just arrived as a freshman in high school, demoralized, and he asked me what the legal age was for dropping out of school. Daniel was not a very good reader, and he knew it, as did everyone else around him. So, from the first days of high school, he refused to read at all and was even starting to find hiding spots in the large building to skip classes.

Daniel had spent years learning to read through *phonics*. This method teaches children the sounds of letters and letter combinations and how to connect those sounds with printed words. As the achievement gap increased between him and his peers, he was subjected to practicing yet more phonics, even on a computer, for more than an hour and a half a day. He missed out on instruction in other subject areas and electives, such as science, social studies, choir, and gym, because learning to read through phonics instruction was of the utmost importance to his parents and administrators.

Everyone wanted Daniel to become a proficient and fluent reader, but he was stuck on learning letter-sound relationships, consonants, vowels, digraphs, blends, diphthongs, syllable patterns, roots, affixes, and each isolated letter or element, one by one in a prescribed sequential manner. As Daniel was learning new letters or linguistic elements, he continued to review old material over and over again, doing worksheets, writing letters in sand trays, practicing with flash cards, and reading low-level books containing controlled words and phrases, such as "Dot

112

has a box for Pam," "In the box are tops," And "Pam likes tops." Daniel had had enough.

When I met Daniel, I told him we were going to read *real* books. He remarked that he liked reading alone at home, but he wouldn't dare to read at school anymore. I assured him that we were not going to do old stuff anymore, especially because he was in high school now. I also asserted that I would not expect perfect reading. He could even read silently to himself, and we would discuss the passage after he was done. I offered Daniel a short passage, letting him know that it was about a wimpy kid needing to find a good breakfast cereal to become stronger for football games. I observed as Daniel grudgingly ripped out a blank page from his notebook and dug out a pencil from deep in his backpack.

Daniel began to read, and when he came upon the word *breakfast*, he copied the word onto his note paper and indicated the vowels by placing a small *v* under each vowel. Then he drew two small swoops between the vowels and made a slash between the consonants *k* and *f* inserted between one of the swoops as a way to break apart the syllables. However, Daniel noticed that there was another swoop (vowel pair *ea*) that didn't contain consonants in between. He wasn't sure what to do but ultimately decided to slash the two vowels. Therefore, he came up with *bre/ak/fast*, pronouncing it as *bree—ack—fast*. Daniel looked up at me and remarked that it didn't make sense to him. So, his second strategy was to copy the entire word again and make small tally marks above each letter, saying each letter and its corresponding sound as he went along: *b-r-e-a-k-f-a-s-t*. Of course, this was not successful either. Giving up, Daniel returned to the passage, skipped *breakfast*, and moved along to *cereal*, beginning with the *c* as a sound, like in *cat*. By this time, Daniel had lost all meaning and was frustrated and anxious. He shoved the passage back toward me and stormed out of the room.

It was definitely time for new literacy practices for Daniel. There is so much more to the process of reading than just phonics. Proficient and fluent readers use multiple strategies (visual, structural, and semantic) to think about and have control over their reading, including setting a purpose for reading, self-correcting miscues, adjusting reading speed, and monitoring comprehension. In other words, good readers think about what looks right, what sounds right, and what makes sense. Often, children who get *b* and *d* or *was* and *saw* mixed up are usually attempting to read letter by letter or word by word without thinking about making meaning. Proficient readers may slow down in trying to read *etiology, entomology, etymology,* or *ethology,* but having some background knowledge of these terms is immensely helpful. And once they know the definition of the term, they may continue to read a passage or a book for comprehension without entirely focusing on each single letter or linguistic element of the words. Proficient and fluent readers also put in a lot of independent practice reading as well.

Daniel put so much effort into reading *breakfast* and *cereal* in isolation, he didn't remember what the passage was about—a wimpy kid who needed to find a good breakfast cereal to become stronger for football games. Reading for meaning can support the decoding just as much as decoding can support reading for meaning. Yet, Daniel's parents insisted that because he was so far behind in his reading, he must continue instruction in phonics. Of course, they became quite skeptical about my role as a literacy specialist, because of my deafness. My inner voice sighed, "Oh, gee. But you're talking to a deaf person who somehow successfully learned to speak, read, write . . . and teach . . . without hearing phonemes. What gives?"

Although I largely got to skip phonics lessons in elementary school, I ran headlong into it during speech therapy. I knew how to read the word *cat,* but I learned later, for the purpose of learning how to speak, that the word was a set of sounds I could not hear: *c—a—t.* I started out being exposed to the *look-say method* of learning to read, with words posted all over my preschool classroom, if only in the form of *look-see.* But I was also exposed to the concept of phonics while learning to make speech sounds from written words. Not long after that, I had to confront the concept that not all English words are spelled the way they are spoken. Additionally, saying multisyllabic words was particularly vexing for me. How does one go about saying words like *etiology, entomology, etymology,* or *ethology*? What a confusing world of English! No matter, I developed a strong sense of *metalinguistic awareness*; that is, an awareness of the internal rules that govern language and the components of language.

Metalinguisitcs does not involve just phonology, but also morphology, syntax, semantics, and pragmatics. My metalinguistic understanding did not come naturally for me. I had to be directly taught how the English language works, so that I could use it. And I had, and continue to have, hours and hours of independent reading practice. However, metalinguistics doesn't come naturally for many people with normal hearing either, for most people learn to speak and read with hardly a second thought. In fact, many people with normal hearing confront issues of metalinguistics when they try to learn a second language, take grammar courses, or when they have a child, like Daniel, who struggles to learn to read.

When I am told that a person has dyslexia, I always ask what it means to that individual. Of course, they are aghast, as if I, the literacy specialist, don't know what dyslexia means! In my defense, this is akin to announcing to a physician that one has cancer. A physician will invariably ask what that means. There are many forms, stages, prognoses, and treatments of cancers. Likewise, there are many theories on what the exact nature of dyslexia really is. Furthermore, there are brain research studies seeking the biological basis of dyslexia. Currently, *dyslexia* is vaguely defined as a developmental reading disability, presumably congenital and perhaps hereditary, that may vary in degree from mild to severe. Dyslexia occurs in people who have adequate vision, hearing, intelligence, and general language functioning. Some researchers and educators, including myself, believe that dyslexia may be due to a lack of quality literacy instruction and meaningful practice in the first place.

Contrary to what most people think, dyslexia is not as simple as reading reversals, such as *b* versus *d* and *was* versus *saw*. Some people think that dyslexia is due to an inability to process sounds and associate them with letters. Yet many deaf and hard of hearing children and children with auditory processing issues can and do learn to read in a timely manner. It seems justifiable to consider *phonemic awareness* (the awareness of the sounds of letters and letter combinations) as a cause of reading acquisition, but it may also be a consequence of reading acquisition. Children can surely learn about some letter-sound relationships before learning to read, but many continue to refine their understanding of letter-sounds relationships *while* learning to read. Teaching children the ABCs in the form of one letter per week, using magnetic letters on the refrigerator, or even in prescribed phonics programs, *prior* to learning to read is not always predictive of reading proficiency and fluency or always effective, as we saw with Daniel and myself.

Many children who are thought to have dyslexia are referred for phonics instruction, such as the Orton-Gillingham approach, which has been in use since the 1930s. Most phonics instruction are prescribed, intensive, highly structured, and sequential, in that they teach the basics of word formation before whole meanings. The programs provide multi-sensory instruction, in that they encompasses visual, auditory, and kin-esthetic (physical) modalities of learning. For example, a child is taught to see a letter, say its name and sound, and write it in the air or in a tray lightly filled with sand. Prescribed phonics programs are controversial with inconsistent research results. Additionally, significant research has been done on young children's emergent literacy, beginning reading development, and how proficient and fluent readers are actually able to read during the past eighty years since prescribed phonics approaches were developed. After all, if a phonics approach worked for all children, we would not have a literacy crisis in which more than a third of our nation's children are reading below grade level. Thus, my inner voice groans, "Oh, gee" every time parents or administrators blindly insist on using phonics instructional methods that were initiated three genera-tions ago and largely have remained unchanged after decades of new research.

When I'm told that a student like Daniel might have dyslexia, I always wonder about what kinds of opportunities the student had for engaging, motivating, authentic, and language-rich reading lessons and practice. Even though the message in my first book is about *opportunity gaps* in literacy instruction, I have been declared a "smug and deluded phony" by insistent parents and angry advocates, who sense that I do not embrace the phonics instruction so seemingly necessary for children identified as having dyslexia, specific learning disabilities, or a develop-mental reading disorder. The actual truth is that I do support phonics instruction, but only in a connected and meaningful manner, using real books and other written material. And only when the instruction is well matched to the individual need of the emerging or developing reader. My concern is that if we are teaching children to analyze single letters and words and nothing else, we are not teaching *reading*. Instead, we may even be unwittingly *creating* dyslexic readers. Besides, the reading wars waged between proponents of teaching phonics first versus proponents of teaching whole language, like the use of flash cards, round-robin reading, and weekly spellings tests, has been long over for both literacy researchers and highly trained literacy specialists.

Instead of pushing labels, classifications, and categories, such as *dyslexia*, and the corresponding approach or program, to the forefront, we should be looking at the needs of the emerging or developing reader by acknowledging that everyone learns differently, even when the targeted outcomes are identical. It is important to acknowledge that learning to read and reading are indeed complex and lifelong processes. They do *not* occur naturally or instinctively like learning language. In order to be proficient and fluent readers, people need to be aware of and use multiple strategies, including automatic word recognition of irregularly spelled words, phonetic and morphological analysis, sentence structure and phrasing, and contextual cues. It certainly helps that there is background knowledge of the text topic and strong language skills.

I started teaching Daniel how to put his finger on tricky words, so that he could read ahead, go back, and use context strategies for figuring them out. I taught him that reading is not an exacting process and that comprehension was the ultimate goal. I taught him how to find small words (e.g., roots, prefixes, and suffixes) inside long words. I taught him that the rules of English don't apply in all situations. I taught him to try different sounds in the beginning of words, such as *cereal*. I taught him to think about what kind of a word he was trying to figure out, whether it was a noun, adjective, or verb. Most of all, I taught him that a lot of practice reading silently was going to help him become more proficient and fluent over time. In addition, I advised Daniel's parents, his teachers, and his tutors to back off on phonics instruction and expecting him to read aloud in an exacting letter-by-letter, word-by-word manner. When working with dyslexic children, we need to evaluate their use of many types of strategies across various reading tasks to determine which skills are intact or deficient. All readers need to be seen through the lens of their strengths and weaknesses as readers, not by their broad identifications, such as being dyslexic and needing prescribed phonics instruction. Thus, my first question to parents and administrators who insist that a child like Daniel has dyslexia is always "What does dyslexia mean to you?"

DRIBBLING VOWELS

ALTHOUGH THERE might not be much difference between the words *aloud* and *out loud*, there is quite a difference between an adult reading *aloud* to a child and a child reading *out loud* to an adult. An adult sharing a bedtime story is reading aloud, but usually with eagerness and expression, bringing characters to life, providing digressions to the story, and even having a few moments of inquiry and discussion between the pages. And, some words on the pages may be read aloud differently than what was written in print without necessarily changing their meanings, a common occurrence when adults bring stories alive to young children. A child reading out loud to an adult, however, is learning or practicing to read every single word and is often persistently corrected.

Wesley, a fourth-grader, learned from a tutor that knowing the five vowels, *a, e, i, o, u,* and sometimes *y,* in the English language was the key to reading. Thus, Wesley read word by word, checking carefully for the vowels in every single word. Because it is the rare English word without a vowel, a page can contain an overwhelming number of vowels for Wesley to pay close attention to. After all, many proficient and fluent readers can read the following meme, making the rounds on social networking sites, without too much difficulty: "Aoccdrnig to rscheearch at Cmabrigde uinervtisy, it deosn't mttaer waht oredr the ltteers in a wrod are, the olny iprmoetnt tihng is taht the frist and lsat ltteres are at the rghit pclae."

Vowel sounds are pronounced with an open vocal tract, so that the tongue does not touch the lips, teeth, or roof of the mouth. As Wesley focused on the vowels in each word, he struggled to sort out the different sounds they are supposed to make. He kept attempting to pronounce each single vowel in various forms, such as *ah, eh, oh, ooh,* or *uh* without thinking about the word itself. Poor Wesley. Even though he was struggling to read fluently and comprehend, he was determined to read better and took his tutor's lesson to heart. Of course, the tutor had not given much thought to the fact that vowels are difficult to discriminate, are impacted by the preceding or following consonants, and vary widely across dialects. Because Wesley aspired to be a star basketball player when he got to high school, I asked him if he ever got into arguments with his friends about the rules of basketball. When he replied yes, I told him he could look up the rules in a book or online. He agreed with that. I then asked him if he was going to read the vowels when he looked up the rules. "Oh YES!" he replied. I posed my wonderment that if he focused on reading vowels, how would he be able to find the rules he wanted to know? Or was he really going to just read the vowels? Wesley thought for a bit. In the end, it dawned on him that he had been exclusively reading vowels for quite some time. Just reading vowels. With resignation and slouched in his chair, Wesley made a whispered request that I talk to his tutor about this.

By focusing on vowels in reading, Wesley had lost all meaning. Proficient and fluent readers who are bilingual or speak a variation of English, such as African American English, know that the sounds (phonemes) and grammar (syntax) of their spoken language do not always exactly transfer to or match the language presented in text. But Wesley was young and not yet aware of this concept. He only knew that he was not a good reader and that he must learn letters and words in order to read better. Wesley lived in an urban setting with parents who worked long hard hours to support their family, and he spoke African-American English. Like most parents, they valued education and wanted their children to succeed in school. Thus, they used some of their hard-earned money to hire an after-school tutor to help Wesley read better. I agreed to meet with Wesley's tutor, so we could work toward consistency in our support to Wesley. As it turned out, the tutor, in keeping track of Wesley's reading, just like Wesley's classroom teacher, was concerned about the number of sounds at the ends of words that Wesley was omitting as well as mispronouncing—for example, *th* as *d* and *dat* for *that*. Not only that, Wesley was omitting some auxiliary verbs, such as *is, am, are, was,* and *were*, and sometimes using *be* instead. Therefore, she felt that Wesley should learn phonics and pay more attention to individual letters in words. And at that time, they were working on vowels. As a child, I don't remember reading out loud to any of my teachers and having each word recorded, counted, and corrected. Perhaps this may have been a good thing, as I was learning speech and syntax from reading rather than matching what little speech and language I had to the text.

In addition to nouns on manila cards placed by every object in my classroom, my teachers also made sure that *functional* words were a part of my developing language and literacy program. Functional words have very little meaning by themselves but they provide a grammatical relationship with other words in a sentence, such as *and, the*, and *is*. My teacher and mother wrote (and drew a simple picture or two) in a daily journal for me that I took back and forth between home and school. A typical entry might have read: "Today is Tuesday. It is raining. I rode in a yellow bus." If my teacher wrote it, I was encouraged to read with my mother at home and vice versa. Because this went on for more than a year, I began to internalize grammatical patterns almost as naturally as a child who could hear. I still have the collection of journals. What struck me though was that many of the commentaries in the margins of my journal pertained to my developing language and literacy abilities:

> *Sorry about the library book. Deb had hidden it from Jeff* [my baby brother].

> *Chris* [a classmate] *brought the* Cat in the Hat *and* Book of Laughs *to school today—Debbie cried because she thought they were hers. Please show her her copies and see if you can explain it better then.*

> *Good golly, Debbie told us one* **is** *and two* **are**!

Even though I couldn't hear and I couldn't speak very well, I was well on my way to learning the structure of language and becoming a reader and writer, which in turn, helped me learn and practice the structure of language. My speech and language was never perfect when compared to so-called standardized or mainstream English, but it was good enough to be understood most of the time. And it was good enough for me to become a lifelong voracious reader.

Both Wesley and I were part of what some educators would call a *nontraditional* population of students. And we were both considered struggling readers. Although Wesley could hear and had full use of a language, his language did not entirely *match* the language of school and books. I don't hear, and I started out my life with a three-year language gap. However, my common membership in a nontraditional population stops there. I was fortunate to learn my language and literacy—and to be educated—at a time when I was not measured every inch of my way or considered underachieving. Wesley, on the other hand, was assessed on multiple tests, referred for special education, and ultimately, covertly segregated into a resource room for a large block of time in his school day. Being a special education student also subjected Wesley to learning skills, such as phonics and sight words, in an isolated and fragmented manner, using low-level and bland reading material. His language, the language of his family and community, was never acknowledged at school. Instead, a focus was made on teaching him how to read vowels and striving for accurate word-by-word reading.

Accents and syntaxes vary with regions and dialects. Broadly stated, an accent is the way a person sounds when speaking—how she pronounces words or the intonation patterns of her voice. All of us are born capable of both producing and perceiving all of the sounds of all human languages. However, early on, infants learn which sounds are important in their language and which they can disregard. By the time a child is a year old, he or she has learned to ignore most distinctions among sounds that don't matter in his or her language. The older a person gets, the harder it becomes for the brain to learn new sounds that are part of a different language.

Children also learn the rules of language as they listen to and begin to use increasingly complex sentences. These rules, or syntax, deal with the arrangement of words and phrases to create sentences in a language. The bottom line is that people unconsciously or consciously learn the features of languages from being immersed in the languages around them.

Although language and literacy are reciprocal and interrelated, the way we pronounce certain words does not always match how those words look in print, even for speakers of supposed standard or mainstream English. Expecting children to read with exacting one-to-one correspondence places the focus on phonemes and syntax. And it often removes the point of making meaning, thinking, and comprehension. Wesley became a better reader when I helped the adults around him—his parents, tutor, and teacher—realize the discrepancy between what they were expecting Wesley to do and what fluent readers actually do. All children, including Wesley, need plenty of practice reading silently and independently. They need plenty of time listening to adults reading aloud to them. And they need plenty of time to carry on conversations about what they have read. When Wesley learned that spoken language does not always transfer to words in print, and when he had more authentic experiences with reading, he began to enjoy reading more. And the more Wesley read, the more proficient and fluent he became.

Pushing for accuracy in reading out loud only serves to disengage emergent and developing readers, because it makes them believe that the words are much more important than the message. Therefore, adults listening to children can ask themselves how far off the miscued word or phrase is from the meaning. For example, Wesley may adjust the syntax of a sentence, and I may substitute or even avoid saying words, if I don't know how they are pronounced. In some ways, my deafness is an advantage when I work with emerging and developing readers, much like the beloved therapy dogs in classrooms and libraries. I don't catch every single phoneme or syntactical difference my students are reading, but when they recognize that their spoken language doesn't match up with the words in the text, they often ask me about it. When their fingers are stuck on specific words or I see frustration arising, I explain how print works versus how we speak. It is validating for people to have gentle conversations about the multiple forms of languages and dialects in our diverse society. However, it is crucial for young children—and their teachers—to be supported in an emotionally safe exploration of contrasts and variations between spoken and written languages, so that children, like Wesley, can become proficient, fluent, and engaged readers.

A VILLAGE

WE ARE A LOT LIKE dogs when we settle in to read. Dogs often circle around on top of their favorite bedding, pawing or fluffing it, before lying down. Most of us, with books in hand, will do the same. We circle around to find our reading glasses, start the kettle for a cup of tea, fluff our pillows, dim the lights, or put on some music. Or maybe we'll decide to read outside. We'll spread out a beach towel or dig the old camp chair out of the garage. Then we'll circle over to the refrigerator for a cold soda or beer. And the books we choose usually come after circling around and browsing in libraries, bookstores, or online catalogs. No matter, plenty of reading opportunities makes for proficient and fluent reading. And once we are proficient and fluent, reading can be a source of great pleasure, knowledge, and escape.

Cameron and his mother were homeless, but she worked long hours to try to save up for a permanent place to live. Cameron was an only child who never knew his father, and he attended five different schools between first and third grade. Despite his history of homelessness, he had perfect attendance. He was delighted when his mother married a nice man. They finally found a house to live in, and he had his own bed. By then, Cameron had become an inquisitive fourth-grader, loved school, and had a voracious appetite for learning new things. And ask questions, he did. He asked, "How is it that airplanes, bees, birds, and butterflies can fly, but they all have different wings?" He understood that whales use baleens to filter small prey, but wondered, "Was that for stuff coming in or stuff going out?" Another memorable question was "If you aim a rocket to Mars and all the planets are moving around in orbit, how do you figure out what time to send the rocket off?" He knew he drove his mother crazy with his questions, especially the ones that stumped her. He feared driving his brand-new, and beloved, stepfather crazy with his questions, too. His classroom teacher always seemed so busy. His peers never seemed to really care. So he resorted to asking me. Of course, many of his questions stumped me, too.

Cameron was on my caseload in his fourth-grade year. I was his sixth resource room teacher. The notes from his previous school reported Cameron was a "struggling reader" who tended to escape from reading by asking a lot of questions and talking all the time. The report also noted that he appeared to have symptoms of an undiagnosed attention disorder. He qualified for special education as a student with learning disabilities. I saw that Cameron was quite the conversationalist and very curious about everything and anything in the world, but I had difficulty seeing him as having attention issues or learning disabilities. But Cameron was indeed resistant to reading, and I wanted to get to the bottom of why.

I decided to take advantage of his numerous questions. After all, I was curious myself! I found various science books about how things fly, a book on whales, and an online article about exploring Mars. Cameron was happy to look through these materials, but he continued to ask questions and talk. If I tried to hold him accountable for actually reading, he would move on to discussing another topic. I decided not to make him read out loud to me and told him he could read by himself on a beanbag chair. While observing Cameron out of the corner of my eye, I saw that he still wasn't reading. He would flip through the pages and wait patiently until it was time to do the next activity.

Cameron had been tested numerous times at all of his previous schools. It was obvious that he was underachieving in reading. But simple test scores on narrow subsets of reading skills do not tell me what is really going on. When I asked Cameron about how he felt about reading, he just shrugged. In trying to brush me off, he professed that he was good at it and that he even liked to read. So finally, I confronted him as kindly as I could, saying that it was certainly great that he was good at it and that he liked to read, but he wasn't reading at school. What was going on? I also remarked that he asked amazing questions about things in our world and that reading was going to be the key to finding out his answers. Digging deeper, I asked what he does when stuck on words he can't decode or doesn't know. Cameron remarked that he knew his letters and could read words on flash cards. But he added that was why he asked questions all the time, because it was hard to read letters and words really fast in books like the other kids do. I also wondered if he had books or a computer at home and whether he had ever been to the local library. He didn't even know people could keep books at home or that there were libraries outside of school. Cameron said that he liked to watch documentaries on television with his mother, and that was the best way to find out about cool stuff.

Finally, a visiting nurse came to check the hearing and vision of the kindergarteners at the school. Because Cameron had been in five schools in three years and his records didn't show that he had any screening for hearing and vision, I made a special request for her to check on Cameron. It turned out that Cameron needed glasses. Glasses in addition to quality instruction on how to decode unknown words and plenty of books to practice. As I began to gently peel all the layers of Cameron's reluctance to read, I was in a better place to support his literacy growth. Cameron finally caught up with his peers within a few months.

If we want children like Cameron to take off in their reading abilities, we must provide the conditions for them to do so. And we must stop relying on standardized tests scores, such as those reported in Cameron's file, as the sole basis for judging the capabilities of readers. Cameron was considered underachieving, and while moving from school to school, he was put to learn subskills of reading, such as phonics and high-frequency sight words on worksheets and flashcards, in resource rooms. Cameron told me about how easy it was to do word search puzzles, copy spelling words over and over until the tests on Fridays, and make simple consonant-vowel-consonant words, such as *sap*, *cut*, and *bit*, with magnetic letters. He shared how he took turns with other children reading out loud a page or two of easy-to-read baby books. And he emphatically stated that the trick to staying out of trouble was to be quiet as much as possible, which he admitted was the hardest thing for him to do. I couldn't help commiserating with Cameron. I told him that he didn't sound like he had fun reading and that he didn't do much of it either. And all the things he did to learn to read didn't even answer his wondrous questions either. Being deaf, and a naturally curious person myself, my primary source for finding out about "cool stuff" was to read.

Cameron, having a hungry mind, loved to watch documentaries. It was a wondrous source of learning for him. Every day, he would report to me what he had seen the evening before. Although I was not at all concerned about the documentaries Cameron was enjoying, excessive television watching was a widespread concern when I was a child. I know my brother reveled in the shows of the late sixties and early seventies. He was particularly fond of Saturday morning cartoons, such as *The Flintstones*, *The Jetsons*, *The Bugs Bunny Show*, *The Rocky and Bullwinkle Show*, *Scooby Doo*, and *Yogi Bear*. He loved watching *Gilligan's Island*, *The Munsters*, and *Star Trek*. He also adored *Flipper*, *Mr. Ed*, and *Lassie*. Although I tried watching some of these shows, I could never figure out the plot or what made people laugh, for there were no captions available in those days. My family members sometimes tried to explain the shows to me, but the comedic twists and turns were often too fast for anyone to keep me up. I've also had people make inflated claims that "I can surely watch television or movies; it's something you *watch* after all. Surely one doesn't need to hear." I always respond with the advice that they should turn off the sound and see how often the lips are clear on the screen and how often voiceovers are used. Everyone should try it sometime before making such assertions. So instead of attempting to watch television, I'd wander off with a book in hand. My brother who loved television still turned out to be a fine reader in his own right.

Without much television and having no need for the reading logs and incentives that they use in schools nowadays, I had my share of easy reading as a child. I remember reading *Hop on Pop* and *Put Me in the Zoo* over and over again with great exaggeration and silliness. My sweet dog faithfully listened; my younger brother, not so much. My early picture books, with goofy rhymes, were a whole lot of easy fun at first but certainly got old very quickly. So, I moved on to children's literature, which still contained pictures but had much more plot development. I loved the fantastical books by Bill Peet, such as *The Whingdingdilly* and *Huge Harold*, that expanded my knowledge from a concrete world to an imaginary one. Were there really witches and wingdingdillies? Can rabbits really grow to be the size of horses? I read *The Little House* by Virginia Lee Burton, my first experience seeing a perspective from something other than a person. I felt sorry for the charming little house and wondered if that could happen in real life. Now being older, when I spot old houses in big cities, I always remember this book and contemplate how the area was once a meadow or forest. I read *Too Much Noise* by Ann McGovern, being curious about all the quiet noises a house can make and marveling at the wisdom of bringing in boisterous farm animals, one by one.

Many of these books were given to me as gifts by my paternal grandparents, not only for birthdays and Christmases, but also for Thanksgivings, Easters, and just because. It didn't take me long to notice that these books were all published by the Houghton Mifflin Company. When I asked my grandmother about it, she confessed that as an employee of Houghton Mifflin in Chicago, she was high enough in ranking that she was able to help herself to these books from their supply closet. However, this grandmother has told numerous grandiose stories, most of which I have later found to be entirely untrue. Therefore, I remain skeptical as to whether she actually worked for this publisher or not. Regardless, finding that most of my books were published by Houghton Mifflin piqued my interest in how the publishing world functioned. I started to pay attention to the publishers of other books. I learned that an author writes a book, an illustrator may be hired, the book is printed up in a factory elsewhere, and the publisher pays everyone by the number of books sold. This latter concept made me worry that the authors and illustrators of the books in my house didn't get their fair share of the profits; they were people after all, and they and their children needed to eat just like the rest of us. When I asked my grandmother about that, I remember being told that the authors and illustrators don't get very much money for their books, which confused my young naïve mind even further. Just how do they feed themselves and their families if their books were being taken from a supply closet?

Although I certainly didn't feel right about the idea of pilfered books, the books were quite enjoyable to read, and they certainly honed my language and reading skills. In researching the history of children's trade books for this book, I learned that the children's book market began its vigorous growth after the two world wars and became a big business well into the sixties and seventies. In fact, many favorite children's books from that time period are still in print today: *Where the Wild Things Are* by Maurice Sendak, *The Snowy Day* by Ezra Jack Keats, *Mr. Gumpy's Outing* by John Birmingham, *Clifford, the Big Red Dog* by Norman Bridwell, and all of the Frog and Toad stories, such as *Frog and Toad Together*, by Arnold Lobel. As a teacher consultant, I've seen dozens of children who started to learn to read from these books after hearing their parents or other adults read the stories to them over and over again. Eventually, they began to recognize patterns in letters and words and tried to read the books on their own. However, some of my students, like Cameron, had never heard of these classics. They had never had books of their own, been read aloud to, or visited the libraries for story hour.

Neither of my parents, although strong readers, were true bibliophiles, so we didn't make frequent visits to the downtown library or a bookstore. My mother even once asked me with wonderment how I managed to become such an avid reader and book collector on my own. Even though we didn't visit the downtown library very often, the library sent out bookmobiles into the surrounding neighborhood parks or schoolyards on a weekly basis in the summertime. Usually, the bookmobile arrived around the same time as the van from the city recreation department. At the same time that the bookmobile offered library books, the city recreation department provided supervised games and art activities, and both were delightfully followed by the ice cream truck. I don't recall the color or the size of our bookmobile, but I do remember the daunting steps to climb up into it. The inside was lined on both sides, from ceiling to floor, with oak shelving, and the small checkout table was directly behind the driver's seat. I was in awe of this mini-library on wheels! However, it came with one caveat. I could not sit cross-legged on the floor, in the middle of the aisle, and browse through potential titles to take home without other children stumbling over me.

Sitting cross-legged in between tall bookshelves reminds me of my first trip to the original Borders bookshop on State Street in Ann Arbor when I was around eleven or twelve years old. I went downtown with a childhood friend named Amy and her family, and Borders was one of the stores we stepped into. I was brought up never to touch anything in stores unless I was planning to purchase it. It was good advice indeed, because if I didn't hear anyone warn me not to touch, I would have suddenly found myself angrily escorted out, which has happened to me. Imagine my confusion as to how to behave in a bookstore. There were hundreds of books on shelves with only their spines facing outward, and they were *for sale*. Therefore, to my mind, that meant they shouldn't be touched unless I was planning to buy them. I shuffled around until Amy noticed my bewildered state of mind. I explained that I didn't have money and wasn't planning on buying books. She pointed out that I could still look through them, and maybe someday I might want to buy one. I confided that I didn't want to get in trouble. Finally, Amy pointed to the long oak benches set between the bookshelves and remarked that the owners put them there so that people would actually sit down and browse through their books. I started observing both adults and children pulling out books and looking through them before putting them back on the shelves. Nowadays, as an adult, I can easily spend an hour or more wandering through bookstores, gently picking up interesting titles and carefully returning them to their appointed slots. And once in a while, I can still be found sitting cross-legged on the floor in front of bookshelves. In the end, as my immediate family members will attest, I hardly ever leave a bookstore without purchasing an armload full of books.

It surely took a village to raise me as a reader, not just my parents. A village of bookmobiles, ice cream trucks, and recreation supervisors. A village of patient family dogs and doting grandparents. A village of bookstores and friends who wander through them. Furthermore, learning to read and developing literacy is a multifaceted and social process, requiring much practice, that is developed over a lifespan using a wide variety of authentic materials. Tests only measure narrow subsets of reading skills, not whether a child has spent thousands of hours of listening to stories, piles of books to look through and read, and even a pair of glasses. And when a child is found to be lacking in one skill or another, such as letters, phonemes, prefixes and suffixes, or whole words, they are too often directly taught these skills in a fragmented and isolated manner. The reality is that I read every day throughout my entire childhood into my adult years, and Cameron read infrequently. Children who are not reading at home or at school, or are reading without glasses, are simply not reading. And like anything we want to be good at, we must practice. The more a person reads, the more proficient and fluent that person gets. But the more a child is expected to read letter by letter, word by word, out loud, on bland texts, the more the child believes he or she is not a good reader.

PART 6

WRITING

INTRODUCTION: DEFINING WRITING

I write to understand as much to be understood.
—Elie Wiesel

WRITING INVOLVES more than just using correct grammar, spelling, and punctuation with some sort of marking implement on a surface. Although writers record language graphically, they also craft their pieces with an audience in mind. People write for many reasons—in journals, letters, opinion pieces, notes, and lists, as well as creatively. Young children love to scribble and write. They write in sand, on walls, and in soapy bathtubs. They write with crayons, markers, pens, pencils, and their pointer fingers. And they write with glee for all to see and read, placing their work on the refrigerator door with a magnet. Some people write notes to themselves to make better sense of difficult concepts and to remember things, or as an emotional or creative outlet. Deaf and hard of hearing people write too, and they write in English, because American Sign Language does not have a written form.

Something happens to some children as they move up the grades in their school career. They begin to dread writing. Some will refuse to do it altogether. Writing requires a lot of thinking, planning, remembering, and organizing. It is hard work. It takes a sensitive and talented teacher to keep the enthusiasm and momentum for writing going beyond kindergarten. All of us, no matter what age, are more willing to write if our purposes are authentic and we have a real audience.

FINGER PAINTING

WRITING IS A LOT like finger painting—it is a messy endeavor. One can write letters and words on a large sheet of paper with delightfully gooey paint, and the colors will swirl, change, and meld. The paints get all over—on hands, sleeves, noses, and wisps of hair. The paint can even get on walls, door fixtures and other tubes or bottles of paint. Likewise, anyone who writes and publishes his or her pieces knows it is a messy activity as well.

Danielle, a shy fifth-grader who did not like to write, loved to chew gum. She wrote the equivalent of two or three sentences a month, if that. Danielle excelled in reading and was right on grade level in all other subject areas. No one could figure out why she refused to write at school, so the principal suggested that her teacher send her to me.

Upon my first meeting with Danielle, she was chewing gum. When I get to know most children, and they get to know me, I can lipread them pretty well. But lipreading someone who is chewing gum can be difficult. Still, I did not ask her to remove her gum. I asked what was stopping her from writing. Did she feel anxious at the sight of a blank sheet of paper? "No." Would changing the color of the paper help? "No." How about drawing first? Or making a plan? "No." Was it that she couldn't think of anything to write? "No." Was it that her fingers and hand hurt or got tired easily? "No." Was it the spelling and all the punctuation? "No." I even tried asking her to dictate a story I made up myself just to see if she would be willing to put pen to paper for me, and she just shrugged. I was starting to scratch my head. I had a kid, a pencil, and a piece of paper sitting there in front of me, and somehow I needed to get her to start writing, so I could see what was going on.

The next time Danielle came to my office, she was still chewing gum. I hadn't told her about my rule about gum in my office. Instead, I decided to use my hearing loss to my advantage. I explained that I really wanted to get to know her, but I could not lipread her very well with gum in her mouth. Therefore, would she write to me? And write to me she did! I kept asking questions about herself and her family as she wrote; she wrote more than two pages about her three cats, four birds, and an aquarium full of fish. Danielle clearly could write. She had beautiful sentence structure. For the most part, she used correct spelling, capitalization, and punctuation. She even indented her paragraphs! Danielle finally confided to me that she loved to write at home. She had a diary and wrote letters to her favorite aunt. But she was afraid to write at school, because her previous teacher had made her writing messy by marking all over her paper with a purple or green pen. Then she was always asked to write everything all over again.

Just as monumental as when children speak their first words and begin to read, parents are mighty proud when they start to scribble and write on their own, and they are equally chagrined when they find writing on the walls of their homes. Most young children start out their lives loving to scribble, draw, and write. They will proudly demonstrate that they can write their names and constantly beg for the correct letters in words. They ask to write on shopping lists, letters to grandparents, and instructions for building a rocket that can fly off to Pluto. Alas, after a few years of school, many begin to hate it. Absolutely detest it. Some children, like Danielle, will even refuse to pick up a pencil altogether. The reality is that it takes a real knack for a teacher or another adult to navigate the fine line between a child's exploration of writing and developing expectations of legible penmanship, proper usage, and correct spelling. So much to learn and so much to do all at once. Knowing how complicated the writing process is, and through the use of chewing gum, Danielle and I reached a mutual understanding about the ups and downs of writing. We both agreed that writing has so many things going on at once and sometimes it can be difficult and scary.

Writing was a part of my school days as a child. Once in a while, my classmates and I had to write poems of varying types, from acrostics to couplets to haikus. And we had to write a book report or two. However, the writing curriculum back when I was a child was more superficial and based on specific skills, as opposed to producing thoughtful and expressive pieces. We were given a list of spelling words every Monday and by the end of the week, a spelling test. I didn't know how many words were pronounced, so I couldn't simply sound them out. But I recall usually acing these tests, because my ability to remember how words were spelled was better than average. We also received a list of words to look up in our dictionaries. I remember having to write the words in alphabetical order, copy each of the definitions, make a list of their corresponding synonyms and antonyms, and write a sentence or two using each word.

We also had plenty of practice in penmanship, in both print and cursive, using buff-colored manila paper. The paper contained rows of three lines—a solid line on the top, a dotted line in the middle, and a solid line on the bottom—and we wrote our letters and words between these lines. It was frustrating that my monkey's tails turned out goofy, and I couldn't always make a capital Q in cursive. Even today, my cursive is not all that readable to others. However, good spelling and an artistic hand do not automatically make for a good writer. Writing was always difficult if we didn't have a chance to go back and polish our pieces. When we jotted our thoughts down quickly for an assignment, it most often showed up as sloppy writing. In turn, our writing would get all marked up with a red pen. I remember wondering who in my class could write perfectly on the first try.

Not only is writing a messy process, but also expressing oneself on paper is an emotionally vulnerable venture. For some, once the writing is on paper, there is a sense of permanency, that one cannot change one's mind and revise the text later. Writers are also concerned about how an audience, particularly those near and dear, will respond. Writing is by far not a job for thin-skinned people.

Due to several family upheavals during the height of my professional and writing career, I was brought to a complete halt in any attempts to express myself, be it writing letters, emails, professional or papers, or even maintaining my blog, for several years. It was all I could do to make myself write student reports at work. A few years before my major writer's block began, my younger brother died suddenly after a short illness, leaving behind a beautiful wife and three preschool-aged sons. Everyone was shocked and grieved. I was too, but I was also lost and alone in my shock and grief. I couldn't hear at the various family gatherings, the visitation, the funeral, the burial, or at the reception afterwards. There were no accommodations for my deafness, and understandably, members of my family were too distraught to fully help keep me up with the rites and conversations. This experience taught me to make sure that I request accommodations in advance in the future, or at least find a friend not directly involved with the situation to help, so that I could be a viable part of my circle of family and friends.

Therefore, during a second upheaval that involved my daughter, Kara, battling her adolescent demons and finding herself involved in the court system, I tried to make sure I took care of my communication needs. I requested a meeting with the prosecutor to discuss Kara's case and brought my own mother along; however, when I arrived, I unexpectedly found five people in the room. Knowing that I was deaf, they talked directly to my mother instead of me. I could not keep up with the discussion, so I made numerous but futile attempts to stop the meeting. I wanted to request accommodations at a reconvened meeting. Instead, I was told that my request was unnecessary, unreasonable, and after all, the problem was not even about me in the first place. Never mind that it *did* involve me. *I* was the one who dialed 911 and, not being able to hear, left the phone hanging, hoping that help would arrive. Help quickly arrived, but not in the manner that I intended. I couldn't get my communicative needs met by the emergency personnel or at the courthouse in order to support Kara. I felt shamed and silenced. I was numb. And I stopped writing.

Writing can provide an outlet, a source for healing, and sometimes a voice. Even though I fired off an email to the judge overseeing the court and was able to get accommodations in the end, it took more than two years and the hiring of a writing coach before I was slowly able to come back out of my shell. I was not able to write about anything personal for the longest time, so I went in a different direction and wrote and published a book and several articles to share a new way of thinking about diverse and vulnerable children's literacy instruction. And eventually, I returned to my blog. Someone commented on my blog that people who write have big egos. This angered me. Writing is hard work. Perhaps *some* people who write have big egos. They desire fame, prestige, money, or tenure. Or perhaps they just want to tell-all about themselves. Many people, however, write to share their thoughts or experiences. Honestly and authentically share. I have come to see that published authors are brave souls indeed. They deserve flexibility and understanding, and although their work has a specific publication date, their personal thoughts, stories, and opinions are dynamic over time; that is, they continue to fine-tune their ideas and concepts. But I also eventually discovered that I write, because I have very few ways of making myself heard. It might be easier for most people to speak one's thoughts, but writing requires more organization, eloquence, and sophistication. Over time, I found it became easier for me to write than to speak my mind. No matter, I write to point out that *all* of us, even those who have perfect hearing, must *listen*. To me. To other people. To Danielle.

Writing is one of the most cognitively demanding tasks that children and adults perform. It is more than a vehicle for communication; it is a vehicle for learning about our world and ourselves. Writing impels us to make connections, organize our thoughts, and think them through with sequence and logic. Today, it may seem that writing is more challenging than ever before. In some ways, it is because of higher writing standards and expectations. In school, children are encouraged to write narrative pieces with descriptive detail and a clear sequence of events, informative pieces that convey ideas and topics effectively, and even opinion pieces supporting points of view with well-thought-out reasons. In other ways, writing is more inviting and hospitable today, because the writing *process* is now being emphasized. This process requires time to think about, plan, write, revise, and edit, even with peers, before making a final "published" product. The very nature of this writing process is much more forgiving when people fully understand that revising and editing is a natural (and messy!) part of producing quality pieces instead of viewing a draft as simply full of errors to be corrected. I earnestly explained to Danielle that it often takes several revisions to come up with a satisfactory piece, and that it was okay to be messy. Her teacher agreed to stop using markers and instead used a revising and editing checklist, following a writer's workshop model of instruction. As a result, Danielle slowly came out of her shell and began to write in class.

Children and adults, like Danielle and myself, can be found at various points on the spectrum of proficient readers and effective writers during their lives. The ability to write effectively, just like proficiency and fluency in reading, continues to develop and evolve in a nonlinear manner over a lifetime—practiced at school, in the workplaces, and at home—from early childhood to college and beyond. Unfortunately, in our current climate of standardized testing, worry over children having dyslexia or learning disabilities, and a deficit-based model of education, there is little room for children to be delightfully messy. Mistakes, miscues, and errors in school writing are duly noticed, counted, and corrected instead of being viewed as a natural—and messy—part of the writing process. Too often, children who struggle are placed in a lower-level group, segregated for remedial or special education, or otherwise seen as having diminished capabilities to learn. And some, like Danielle, will refuse to write altogether. Thus, they are relegated to resource rooms, where they work in on their best penmanship between the dotted lines, learn phonics in isolation, or practice for a spelling test each week, like in the old days. They have few opportunities to push, to see, to learn, to change, and to grow in the world of words and writing. We need to allow everyone to be the *messiest, exploring-est,* and *growing-est* writers ever!

JIRAF, TUTUL, AND BUNE

WOULDN'T IT BE NICE if we could invent the spelling of the words we want to write? In some ways, young children just learning to write—in the sand, with fat pencils and crayons, and with magnetic letters on the refrigerator—are smarter than we are. English contains such a whimsical and inconsistent system of representing our spoken sounds into letters and words, yet, young children who know the letters and their sounds are perfectly comfortable spelling words the way they sound.

Paige was a second-grader in a multi-grade classroom with peers in first through third grades. The teacher had implemented a literacy workshop model, rather than a reading-writing program, so her students spent their mornings talking, reading, writing, and sharing authentic books and other materials.

I came to observe the teacher and her classroom, because this teacher's records of literacy scores demonstrated the greatest growth in the school district. Here was a gifted teacher who had all of her charges fully engaged in languages and literacies. Instead of desks or round tables in perfect rows, there was a library corner with books scattered all over the floor, on small tables, and on shelves. Near the library was an antique clawfoot bathtub, painted in purple and bathed in sunlight. It was lined with blankets and pillows and always had a child or two snuggled in it with a book. Another corner of the library had a big refrigerator-sized box, painted green and set down on the floor lengthwise, with the entry cut out like a mouse hole. Almost every moment, there would be two or three children inside with pillows and books. Comfortable child-sized seating, from beanbags to camp chairs to rocking chairs, was scattered about, most with a kid and book in it. The children could do research or write on the eight computers lining one of the classroom walls. And there was an old typewriter, just for fun, in the middle.

In the corner across from the library was a table filled with baskets and small shelves filled with writing implements and book-making materials. All kinds of pencils—mechanical, colored, and number 2s—and all

142

colors of fine and fat markers and highlighters were stored in tubs ready for when inspiration struck. There were shelves of various papers—white, colored, lined, cardstock, sticky notes, and even index cards. There were envelopes, short and long, and even manila interdepartmental envelopes. There were pocket folders, file folders, and a variety of blank notebooks and journals. There was a plastic bin full of clipboards for students to place papers in and write on. There were baskets of pencil sharpeners, staplers, scotch tape, paper clips, rulers, hole punchers, glue sticks, and tubes of white-out correction fluid. And on a small table with a single chair in front of it, next to the writing table, was a bin specially designed for spelling. I hadn't noticed this spelling bin before but found that it was filled with dictionaries, picture dictionaries, hand-held spelling checkers, and word lists. It also had magnetic letters and a dry erase board with a dry erase marker attached to it.

I happened to be sitting right next to this spelling bin when Paige came over with a clipboard and the book *Mr. Gumpy's Outing*, a children's story about two children, a rabbit, a cat, a dog, a pig, a sheep, chickens, a calf, and a goat all going for a ride in Mr. Gumpy's boat on the river. Paige announced to me that she knew exactly what to do. She wanted to write and create her own book, like *Mr. Gumpy's Outing*. She was delighted with the ending of this book. Even though the boat flipped because the goat kicked, the calf trampled, the chickens flapped, the sheep bleated, the pig mucked about, the dog teased the cat, the cat chased the rabbit, the rabbit hopped, and the children squabbled, Mr. Gumpy was still nice enough to offer them all tea and cakes.

Paige decided that the first step to writing her own story was to make a list of the animals that were going to ride on *her* boat. Her boat was going to be like her uncle's speedboat, a really fast boat that might even knock all the animals off if they didn't hold on. Paige set down her clipboard on the table. She had already started her list: *jiraf, tutul, bune.* She pulled out the dry erase board and the magnetic letters. Of course, my attention was diverted to her instead of the teacher, wondering what she was going to do with her list and her story. She looked at her first word: *jiraf.* She clapped out two syllables, *jir . . . af.* She wrote *jiraf,* sounding out each letter, on the dry erase board. Then she sighed, glanced over at me, tossed her two long brown braids with red hair ties over her shoulders, and turned back to the bin.

Paige knew that *jiraf* wasn't spelled right, but she didn't quite know how to spell it. She checked the word list for words that began with *j*, but that didn't help her. She picked up a dictionary momentarily but then placed it back in the bin, choosing the small hand-held spelling checker instead. She carefully typed in *j-i-r-a-f*, checked to make sure each letter was in place, and then tapped the Enter key. Suddenly, she jumped up with glee and shouted, "Oh! It starts with a *g*! Giraffe!" She showed the word on the spelling checker to me and wondered out loud how she was supposed to know which letter to use, a *j* or a *g*? And she noted that it had two *f*s and an *e*! Then Paige went back to the next words on her list: *tutul* and *bune*. Using the various resources in the spelling bin, she figured out that *tutul* should be spelled *t-u-r-t-l-e*, and *bune* should be *b-u-n-n-y*. She crossed out the incorrect words on her sheet of paper and created a new list with the corrected words. Satisfied, Paige skipped off to the next step of putting her story together.

Paige was making the developmental transition from invented spelling to conventional spelling. As she was exploring how to spell her list of animal words, she understood that she was venturing into a bewildering world of spoken sounds and their not-so-corresponding letters. It was obvious to me that the teacher had assured the students that spelling can be a particularly arbitrary and perplexing task, so Paige was not at all distressed. Later, the teacher explained to me that she would be a millionaire if she was paid a nickel for every single time one of her twenty to twenty-four students asked how to spell a word. Therefore, at the beginning of the school year, she taught them how to use the spelling bin as a resource and encouraged them to try it first before asking her.

Spelling was, and still is, particularly difficult for me, because I don't always know how words are pronounced. However, once I know the correct spelling, I usually have a good memory for it. I couldn't help but wish I had a spelling bin in my classroom as a child! What an awesome concept!

Back when I was a child, we didn't have word lists, dry erase boards, or technology, such as hand-held spelling checkers, computers, and word processors, in our classrooms. Instead, we had spelling bees, games of hangman, and clunky dictionaries. And we all knew who in our classes were good spellers and who were not. In spelling bees, I had trouble lipreading the words for me to spell, for they were always announced in isolation and vexed with *visemes*. A viseme is a group of speech sounds that look alike on the lips and mouth when lipreading, such as (*m, b, p*), (*t, d*), and (*f, v*). Similarly, words can be *homophenous*; that is, they look alike to lipreaders. For instance, if you look in the mirror and say *mat*, *bat*, and *pat* without using your voice, you won't see any difference.

Even though we were not given simple homophenous words for the spelling bee, it was still difficult to lipread longer multisyllabic words. Sometimes the teacher would say the word in a sentence, but more often than not, I still wouldn't catch the word. My classmates would laugh uproariously when the teacher gave me a word to spell and then heard me spell an entirely different word. Sometimes my speech sounded like a different letter than I intended. Outwardly, I would try to laugh along, but internally, I was always confused, demoralized, and embarrassed. My classmates would also lose patience as the teacher tried to get me to lipread, so that I could try to spell the correct word. Of course, the teacher couldn't write the word down for me to read and then spell! That wouldn't be fair to the other kids. However, I always wondered why teachers couldn't just show each one of us a picture instead of announcing each word. Wouldn't the playing field be more level for all of us then? There was still a chance that I wouldn't know how a word was pronounced in order to try to sound it out, but at least, I wouldn't fail every single word on my turn.

Hangman was only a little bit easier. During the game, we took turns guessing a letter, but each letter would be written on the chalkboard, either as part of the unknown word or over on the side, if it was not part of the unknown word. However, I was not able to hear if other kids blurted out what they thought the word might have been. So, if I called out a guess and someone had already tried it, I would see eyes rolling and groans. I could not participate in the process of elimination. Whereas today, I am quite hard to beat in a game of Scrabble, Words with Friends, or Bananagrams, I was miserably known as a child who was squarely in the bad speller category.

My difficulties were not necessarily from an inability to spell per se but from simply not hearing. Even if it didn't seem that way to my teachers and peers, I had a pretty good grasp of letters and words from my years of intervention, direct teaching, and speech therapy. My first recollection of understanding the similarities and differences between speech and print involved the word *stopped*. For a time, I had been pronouncing *stopped* literally, with a final *d* sound. I would also try to pronounce *boys* with an *s* instead of the *z* sound. Until someone pointed this out to me, it never occurred to me that *stopped* is pronounced as *stop-t* and *boys* as *boy-z*. Nowadays, it is not uncommon for me to read my students' spelling of words based on the sounds that they hear rather than how it is conventionally spelled. They often spell *stopped* as *stopt* and *boys* as *boyz*. I constantly tell my beginning and developing readers and writers countless times: "Sometimes English is a funny language!"

Spelling is a task requiring some knowledge of letter–sound relationships, a good memory, and a set of resources. Jingles, such as "i before e, except after c" do not always work, not only because there are so many exceptions to the rule, but also because spelling has been viewed in isolation from its historical and linguistic roots in languages.

Unfortunately, spelling is often a huge roadblock for people in their attempts to write. In some languages, like Finnish, Italian, and Spanish, the relationship between letters or symbols and spoken sounds is fairly consistent and takes less time for children to learn. However, English, a derivative of multiple languages, is a spoken and written language with many inconsistencies and exceptions. In fact, Theodore Roosevelt, George Bernard Shaw, Benjamin Franklin, Noah Webster, Mark Twain, and many other prominent people have challenged the conventional spelling of words in English, and some even have called for spelling reform.

Some people may be concerned that technology is decreasing our collective spelling abilities, especially with regard to texting or other electronic communication. But *textism*, the use of abbreviations, acronyms, single letters, and symbols while texting messages, is actually another form of language, literacy, and discourse. Textism is learned over time, just like writing and spelling in English, much to the chagrin of older adults trying to decipher what their grandchildren might be saying. "LOL," "OMG," and "TTYL" aside, textism is much different than when we write in a more formal context. Therefore, spelling checkers, electronic dictionaries, and word prediction software can make or break a person's willingness to put together a narrative or expository piece, a formal letter, and so forth. Of course, such tools are not a panacea, but a resource. We must know some letter–sound relationships and basic patterns of our English orthographic system in order to use the tools. For instance, Paige knew that *jiraf* contained two syllables and that there should be a vowel in each syllable. Additionally, we must also be aware of the particularly sneaky *homophones*, words that have the same pronunciation but are spelled differently and have different meanings. I truly think that Paige's teacher got it right. Make lists, scribble thoughts down, and put together a first draft or two, but then seek ways, using a wide variety of resources, to spell the words correctly, so that the piece is there for all of us to enjoy.

"'NOTHER STINKIN' 'SIGNMENT"

TEACHABLE MOMENTS, when teachers seize upon the ideal time to offer an opportunity for insight, analysis, or critique, are usually wonderful and even enlightening . . . until one has to *write* about it. Then it becomes another stinking assignment.

Jamison, who was the size of a football player and who positioned himself as the gentle class clown, attended an alternative high school for students needing flexible scheduling, project-based learning, internships, GED courses, or simply a smaller academic environment than a larger traditional high school. When the history teacher, Mr. Brown, introduced their next unit about the history of women in our country, he told the class he wanted them to learn about little-known but notable or influential women of color, such as Sally Hemings, Henrietta Lacks, Ruby Bridges, Shirley Chisholm, and the women who worked behind the scenes as "human computers" at NASA to send American astronauts into space.

In the course of a short discussion about marginalization, a student asked what the difference was between apathy, empathy, and sympathy. Seeing it as a good question, Mr. Brown attempted to turn this into a teachable moment. He listed these words on the white board with a bright-red dry erase marker. Jamison blurted out with exasperation, "Uh oh. Here comes a 'signment." Mr. Brown ignored him and asked everyone to pull out their phones, tablets, or laptops to look up the three words using Google and write their definitions in their notebooks. He gave them fifteen minutes to do this task. Jamison breathed a loud sigh of relief and said , "Ok, a li'l 'signment. We can just copy this stuff down." The entire class grumbled quietly, but everyone got to work. It was just a little assignment after all; only three words and three definitions.

When the fifteen minutes was up, Mr. Brown called on one student to recite a definition for *apathy*. Of course, Jamison declared, "That's 'xactly what I'm feelin' right now! I don't care about definitions!" Mr. Brown called on another student to provide the definition of *empathy* and a third student the definition of *sympathy*. Jamison vented that Mr. Brown had no empathy for his feelings about his dire situation in his history class and that he deserved some sympathy for his misfortunes in needing the required credits in order to graduate, eliciting some mild chuckles among his classmates. Mr. Brown continued to ignore Jamison but devilishly decided his students should write a paragraph using real-life examples involving women they know for each definition. At this point, Jamison really began to get worked up: "Not 'nother stinkin' 'signment! Why can't we just talk about our women? You keep giving us extra assignments on top of assignments!"

Even though Jamison's complaints could have gotten him kicked out of the classroom or lodged in the principal's office, he was on to something here. Writing spontaneously for an assignment is an entirely different matter than writing for narrative or expository purposes. Writing is hard work. It involves thinking about and keeping track of many things. Writing requires setting a clear purpose and keeping the audience in mind. It usually starts out with scribbling notes and doing research. It entails thinking ideas through and developing a plan, outline, or narrative arc. And it requires coming up with a good topic sentence, using good supporting details, and crafting a conclusion in well-organized paragraphs.

Writing also calls for visualizing and choosing descriptive words like adjectives, verbs, and metaphors, as well as trying to write what one means to say. It also involves forming letters and words using good penmanship or typing, plus remembering to capitalize, punctuate, indent, keep track of grammar, and use the same tense throughout. Writing means figuring how words are spelled, especially when they don't look like how they are pronounced, like *thought, dough, drought, hiccough,* and *enough*. It can include citing references and dealing with irritating bugs in word processing software. Writing entails drafting, discarding, and starting over. Writing involves being subjected to a peer reviewer's thoughts and an editor's pen. And revising. And revising. And revising. I know, because I've been there. Fifty-something thousand words, 110 pages, and 186 references later, my first book was finally published.

I didn't start out intending to be an author. Years ago, my friends, colleagues, and family who know me well told me I should write a book about my unique educational experiences and how I learned to read and write. So, I started to keep notes in journals, on scrap paper and sticky notes, on my Facebook page, and on my computers. I clipped articles and research papers from newspapers and professional journals. I spent time at university libraries. And I started writing a few narratives here and there before I finally published my first book, but one that did not answer the burning question of how I learned to read and write. Many people still believe in the outdated notion that deaf people are not able to read, much less able to write, past a fourth-grade level. Yet, reading and writing—strengthening and deepening language and literacy—are processes that a person, with or without disabilities, develops over a lifetime.

Knowing that writing is indeed a messy process, I turned my grown-and-gone son's bedroom into an office space. I set up an old card table but soon realized that this was not enough space for the scattered papers, articles, notebooks, books, and laptop computers. I found in my beloved neighbor's barn a brown four-by-four-foot sheet of Masonite board and hauled it into my office and placed it on top of my card table. Even though this extra space was helpful, I still had papers, articles, notebooks, and books scattered all over the floor. Atop the Masonite board in the midst of all my piles, there was a jar of pencils, markers, highlighters, and a pair of scissors. Next to that jar was another jar of colored pencils for me to fill in coloring book pages as I paused to think. And there was a third jar containing chocolate chips to keep me fortified.

I wrote my book and several articles, because I wanted to share a new way of thinking about diverse and vulnerable children's literacy instruction. I was not after fame or prestige. I knew at the start that this book would not go on any bestseller list. I was not after money. I have made only $58 for the three years I worked on this project. I was not part of a university, so there was no need for tenure. I went through numerous templates, outlines, revisions, and editorial processes before it was finally all said and done. Every page had to be thought out, organized, and reflected upon. And every single word, phrase, and line was subjected to an editor's pen. Every citation had to be checked and rechecked.

There were days I wrote twenty words, and there were days I wrote 1,000 words. And there were days I sat in front of my Masonite-covered card table and just cried with weariness and frustration. There were even a few times when I packed up my entire office into boxes and announced to my husband, Klaus, I wasn't going to write another word and vacuumed the floor. But after taking a break for a week or so, I would figure out how to reorganize the project and would be ready for another fresh start. This was a book I had to finish, especially considering that I had deadlines to meet. As Jamison would put it loudly and clearly, the whole idea really was a stinkin' 'signment! However, I did want to get my book, and my message, out.

Writing is a sociological phenomenon. Although the process of writing adheres to definite rules of discourse and grammar, it is not instinctive like spoken language. After all, writing holds a less central place in the history of the human species. No community has ever been found to lack a spoken or signed language, but few languages have ever been written down. In the context of human evolution, writing is fairly new, only about 6,000 years old. Nor is writing simply language written down, because the formal features of writing are quite unlike those found in spoken or signed language. Instead, writing is structured by the conventions of lettering, symbols, punctuation, and the use of space on paper or another surface. Often, the kinds of sentences that occur in writing bear only an indirect relationship to the more free-flowing and complex structures of spoken and signed languages. Additionally, writing does not contain intonation and gesture. Furthermore, writing is not the flip side or the reverse of reading.

Decoding (reading) and *encoding* (writing) both involve working with a common base—the sound-symbol systems we use in text to represent a language; however, they entail different cognitive processes in order to be successful. Both require some phonemic awareness (the awareness of sounds/phonemes that make up spoken words). Even though I do not hear speech sounds, I have the awareness that such sounds exist and are connected to symbols, such as letters and words.

When proficient and fluent readers decode, they adjust their reading in a linear and nonlinear manner according to the difficulty of the text, their background knowledge and life experiences, the depth and breadth of the vocabulary, and their purposes for reading (for pleasure, to learn something new, or even for a test). They note when they mis-cue a word, a phrase, or even a paragraph by rereading, self-correcting, inferring, or looking up definitions. And they monitor themselves for comprehension.

Writing effectively is a much more laborious process, one that includes thinking, planning, drafting, revising, and editing in a recip-rocal and interrelated manner. It is a process in which a person may be thinking about one thing, such as formulating a coherent sentence, and unintentionally omitting other things, such as correct spelling or punctuation. At the same time, it doesn't mean that reading and writing are entirely separate enterprises; they are, in fact, reciprocal and interre-lated in many ways. Someone who reads a lot will be exposed to many different genres, structures, complexities, and styles, as well as a large vocabulary and more in-depth knowledge, all of which support better writing skills and written expression. And when a person writes notes while reading, whether in the margins, in notebooks, in citations, or even in critiques or reviews, the material is comprehended more deeply.

Ultimately, people like Jamison, his teacher, and his classmates need to be aware of the sociological conventions and construct of writing. They all need to know that it is unreasonable for a spontaneous "stinkin' 'signment" to be written effectively or perfectly the first time. It should be okay to just get stinkin' stuff down on paper, and if it is a required or desired project, to plow through the steps in the longer process of writing a final piece.

MARGINALIA

SOME READERS give a book or other media their full attention by hovering over it with a sharpened pencil. The active processes of underlining, scribbling comments, annotating, inserting questions, listing, numbering, graphing, doodling, and sketching can deepen thinking and understanding of the information presented in a text, or even a lecture or video. One early Saturday morning in April of 2015, Rileigh, along with more than one million other viewers, observed a livestream of April, a thirteen-year-old giraffe, giving birth to her fourth calf.

Gestation in giraffes can last anywhere from thirteen to fifteen months. During April's last few months of gestation, people anxiously and impatiently watched as she paced in her stall, leading many to believe that her pregnancy was faked as part of a conspiracy theory or even as an April Fool's joke. Some people were even driven to the point of mild insanity for having wasted so much time watching a very pregnant giraffe walk around in circles.

Rileigh, a precocious first-grader, wanted to know how giraffes are born and decided on her own that she would make a record of April's labor. She found several blank sheets of paper and started with a title page in purple and green markers: "April will have her baby!" Rileigh then got a pencil to write notes in large one-inch letters. She placed lines in between each stage of the birth.

April is holding her tail up

More of the babys legs are coming out

April is licking the baby

April is pacing alot

The dad is checking on April and the baby

The baby is moving

The baby has a sac on it

Rileigh wrote entries throughout the entire labor until the calf was born, delightfully ending her set of pages with a final announcement: "It is a boy!" Most notes or lists are brief and quickly jotted down in margins and on post-it notes, notepads, and pieces of scrap paper to serve as memory aids. However, notes, annotations, and sketches can also be made to help process complex information in the material; the note-taker or reader can mark important points, ask questions, write definitions, make connections, and even challenge concepts or opinions. Rileigh was at an age where many children are trying to figure out where babies come from. She simply wanted to write it down, so that she could make sense of what she was observing on the zoo's webcam. Even at such a young age, Rileigh is surely on her way to college.

In contrast to taking notes while listening to a lecture or a video, *marginalia*—making personal marks in the margins of books—is a way of closely attending to or even collaborating with an author. Reading someone else's margins in books or texts provides an intimate window into such interactions between the reader and author. Of course, the practice of marginalia in textbooks is discouraged in educational settings and libraries. Books must be preserved for the next reader. No one likes books that are covered with distracting underlines and highlights. Although juggling lipreading and writing or watching sign language and taking lecture notes at the same time can be difficult, I have been questioned numerous times whether I was even capable of reading written material, such as books, papers, syllabuses, or handouts, and taking notes. With this assumption gone too far, I am often asked how was it possible for me to make it through high school and college without taking *any* notes, especially in the days before computers, captioning, and internet search engines. The reality is that I would have not made it through my educational or professional career without writing extensive notes, annotations, and even marginalia.

In meeting the science requirements for a high school diploma, I was too squeamish to take biology, so I took earth science instead. This course covered geology, hydrology, and meteorology, with an emphasis on Michigan and its surrounding great lakes. The five large freshwater lakes, Superior, Michigan, Huron, Erie, and Ontario, formed at the end of the last glacial period when retreating ice sheets exposed their basins and filled them with meltwater. Michigan also has many inland lakes and rivers.

I learned how the geology of the area, including kames, kettles, eskers, drumlins, moraines, and escarpments, were formed from the glaciers. I learned about the classes of rocks—sedimentary, metamorphic, and igneous—and how they were formed. I learned about watersheds and different parts of rivers, such as tributaries, flood plains, meanders, oxbows, mouths, and wetlands. I learned that the water cycle involves evaporation, transpiration, condensation, precipitation, surface run-offs, and groundwater. I wouldn't have learned as much as I did without strong listening strategies and study skills. I began with lipreading the lectures as much as I could, and yet, at the same time, I was fully aware of how much information I was missing. I couldn't catch everything when teachers paced back and forth in front of the class, turned their backs to write or draw something on the chalkboard, or parked themselves in front of the overhead projector.

When I experienced gaps in my understanding, I made sure to leave a blank space in my notes. I also paid attention to signals that something might be important. As soon as I lipread transitional words, such as *first*, *second*, and *third* . . . or phrases, such as *remember that* . . . or *on the other hand*, I increased the intensity of my focus on lipreading the material about to follow. Sometimes, I would catch the concept of something, such as a description of how sand is deposited at the mouth of a river, but not the key word, such as *delta*. Other times, I would lipread the key word, such as *barometric pressure*, several times but still not understand the concept.

Even if I did not understand both the vocabulary and the corresponding concepts, I still wrote what I could in my notes and placed a question mark in the gaps. I also watched for body language, such as pointed fingers, more forward and assertive postures, gestures of emphasis, or mouth movements that seem clearer or louder. If the body language was relaxed and the teacher seemed to be just chatting away with examples or digressions, I took those moments to jot my notes down. Of course, my notes on wide-ruled loose-leaf notebook paper were quite messy.

I also brought along sheets of carbon paper to my classes. I asked one or two of my peers on either side of me if they would be willing to let me stick carbon paper, along with an extra sheet of paper, under their paper, so that I could have copies of their notes. Most of my classmates were more than willing to share their notes, especially as we matured and they realized it was about my access to the lectures rather than cheating the system. In order to not inconvenience the notetakers next to me, I tried to be quick to provide a new sheet as soon as they turned the pages of their notebooks, even while trying to take my own notes. Before leaving the class for the day, I made sure I had my own notes, carbon copies of my classmates' notes, all of the handouts from the teacher, and my textbook bundled together and placed in my backpack.

Upon returning home, I laid out all of my notes and reading materials. Then, I got a pair of scissors, cut my own notes into strips, and carefully set them back in order on the floor or my bed. Next, I cut apart the notes from my peers, sorted them, and placed them in the gaps of my own notes. I also cut apart my handouts. I made sure to look up and write down the definition of every unknown word on a piece of scrap paper. Then I inserted the definitions and concepts in the appropriate slot between my strips of notes.

Because I couldn't mark up my textbooks, I lightly penciled in a code, such as an asterisk, star, or checkmark, in the margins and placed a matching code in the margins of one of the strips of notes. I scribbled small notations or underlined in the books when necessary. Finally, when everything made sense to me, I neatly rewrote my notes in a spiral notebook. And I went back to carefully erase all the marginalia I made in my textbooks. If something still did not make sense, I checked in our family's set of encyclopedias or researched the topic in the school library. If my own research wasn't satisfactory to my understanding, I placed a question mark by the gap in my notebook, so I could remember to ask my teacher after class or after school. Asking was a last resort, because I worried about bothering my teachers or even finding myself removed from the school for being seen as incapable of mastering the curricular requirements.

It seemed to me that my method of gathering notes and learning was a tremendous amount of work, but at the same time, I appreciated my learning experiences. I acquired a good set of study skills and, in turn, was able to pass most tests and write papers, even without overnight cramming sessions. Decades later, I can still remember some of the things I learned in high school. However, other classes I took, like literature, were not conducive to taking notes, because the teacher and students carried on a book-club type discussion. In these kinds of classes, I noticed that most of my peers would not take notes either; they simply listened or joined in the debates or dialogues. It was in situations like this that I would start counting ceiling tiles, looking at the variety of shoes, and observing insects crawling across the floors.

Much to my chagrin, I found out that some of my peers did not even read the required books at all. They would listen to the discussions and still be able to answer essay questions at the end of each chapter. Because I couldn't keep up with the discussions, I had to read the books. It may have seemed unfair, but I treasured the time I spent reading *Beowulf*, *A Midsummer Night's Dream*, *Of Mice and Men*, *To Build a Fire and Other Stories*, *The Old Man and the Sea*, and *To Kill a Mockingbird*. Marginalia, of course, was not allowed in school-issued books. However, I would make notes of interest with their corresponding page numbers in my spiral notebook. Sometimes, essay questions were given out before the required reading, so I would copy the questions in my notebook and make preliminary notes before writing the essays on the worksheet. A tremendous amount of note taking and writing on my part was probably the key to my success in my educational career.

As Rileigh discovered and I have known for decades, writing down definitions, concepts, classifications, and commentaries deepened our understanding, and the skills of listening, attending, and note-taking were a source of empowerment toward our personal, educational, and professional growth throughout our lives. Unfortunately, technology has resulted in more passive approaches to learning. As a result of the historical shift from industrialization to an economy based on digitalization and computerization, we are now living in an overwhelming information age. Many teachers and professors pass out copies of their notes, and many who attend lectures receive copies of PowerPoint presentations.

Some people are expert typists and can type nearly everything being said verbatim. Other people use their smartphones to take pictures of quotes, tables, and figures. Some people even record lectures and discussions with their tablets. And people simply Google information. Too often, information is gathered without giving it much further thought. Much of it is rarely reviewed and ends up in recycling or trash bins, both physical and virtual. Somehow, Rileigh knew to take an active approach to the wondrous technology of webcams by making notes, rather than just sitting and passively watching the giraffe birth.

It is not the technology itself that is causing passivity, but the lack of active conscious cognitive processes in which people summarize, classify, analyze, synthesize, critique, connect, and apply available information. I am not turning my back on technology. Captioning has made a whole world of difference for me in accessing lectures and media. Google and other internet search engines allow me to define words and look up information more easily. Yet, I still take notes by hand or by using my laptop computer in a productive manner. I still sort out, make meaningful connections, and determine the usefulness of data and information at hand. Keen competence in listening, attention, and organizational skills, even through written notes and marginalia, is vital toward mindfulness and well-being in both personal, educational, and professional lives.

PART 7

LITERACIES

INTRODUCTION: DEFINING LITERACIES

The bond between the book reader and the book writer is a tightly symbiotic one.

—NICHOLAS CARR

IN A CULTURALLY and linguistically heterogeneous society, the definition of *literacy* is complex, controversial, and dynamic, and it does not always mean "being educated." Furthermore, limiting a definition of literacy to a basic, or "functional," ability to read and write is archaic. A rigid dichotomy between literacy and illiteracy shows the potential for injustice and discrimination. After all, literacy falls on a spectrum, and there are many types, such as intergenerational literacy, cultural literacy, computer literacy, media literacy, academic literacy, and workplace literacy. And there are many genres and overlaps of genres, including biographies and autobiographies, creative nonfiction, mysteries, science fiction, fantasies, adventures, comics, romance and pulp fiction, poetry and prose, drama, self-help, cookbooks, and research papers.

The currently accepted definition is that literacy is an interaction between social demands and individual competence, but it is futile to develop a single definition of the word. It is more empowering and inclusive to describe practices around print as *literacies*. Certainly, deaf and hard of hearing people are immersed in many forms of literacies. When we embrace multiple literacies, we can find strengths for learning, culture, identity, and productivity in all of us.

NOSY

NOSINESS AND GOSSIPING seem to go hand in hand. We are all familiar with a person who wants to know every detail of people's comings and goings, thoughts and feelings, personal business, and misfortunes. Nosy people are so unsatisfied with their own lives, they persistently feel the need to butt in and interfere with someone else's life. Sometimes a nosy person needs to feel a sense of superiority and sets out to find ways to put another person down by looking for faulty characteristics or bad news. No matter, after a nosy person has dug for more information, he or she puffs up with power and pride with the latest knowledge.

Addison was a seventh-grader who had struggled to read to the point where she refused to even try anymore. Petite for her age, she was very reserved, soft spoken, and because she was so introverted, she managed to slip through the cracks at school. Everyone knew that she scored poorly on tests but always thought it was because of her meekness. She seemed capable of functioning well enough in her academic classes, so her teachers were not worried.

Like many people who struggle with literacy, Addison had developed a knack for diverting herself from the task of reading and not letting on to her teachers or peers that she wasn't reading. She carried books around and pretended to read. She listened carefully, filled out worksheets by furtively looking over and copying from her peers, and used dictation software to write on her tablet. She was good at math calculation but struggled with story problems, so she would look for numbers and simple words, like *add, and, subtract*, or *times*, and take a good guess. Many times, she would just wait until the teacher was ready to go over the problems with the class, and then she would mark the correct answers on her papers before turning them in.

Addison kept up with the news and latest fads by browsing the media and websites, like youtube. Unfortunately, because she was diagnosed as a student with learning disabilities and promoted in every grade, she even fooled her parents. In every way, she seemed like a normal teenager, except that she was in special education and could not read or write very well.

In seventh grade, Addison's homeroom teacher, Mr. Morgan, was not fooled. He knew the tactics that some people use to hide the fact that they don't read. He knew that Addison was one capable and sharp kid. He knew that most people with disabilities have normal cognitive abilities. And he didn't believe that a disability was an excuse for not reading proficiently and fluently. On top of that, Mr. Morgan knew that the term *learning disabilities* had no clear definition. In his mind, there was no reason that Addison shouldn't be able to read and write. So, he called me, as a literacy consultant, for help.

After slowly building Addison's trust, I found that she knew many letters and words in isolation. She had learned how to take apart multisyllabic words by marking a *v* under each vowel, making a swoop between each vowel, and then making a slash between the consonants, so that she could sound out each syllable and then eventually put the entire word together. She also would put her finger under every single word and read out loud to herself. But Addison noticed that other people didn't read like she did, and she developed a narrative that she was, in her words, *dumb* and *stupid*. She stopped trying and finessed her way through school without having to do any actual reading.

After a few weeks of restorative literacy sessions with me, in which I taught her how to read the way *real* readers do, Addison began to pull everything together and build her confidence again. A whole new world opened up for her. She became quite nosy and began to read everything that was in her path. She snooped on emails left open in laptops, forgotten documents in copy machines, notes scattered on office counters and desks, papers in clipboards carried by the principals, and journal pages on student desks. She read notes being passed among her classmates and got caught reading her older sisters' diaries. She was even caught going through her father's business letters and invoices in his den. Her parents joked that her newfound confidence in reading might be a mixed blessing. In time, however, Addison happily moved on to reading comics, graphic novels, magazines, and chapter books.

Literacy is a form of social construct. It provides communication and connection between authors and readers. And it expands a person's world of knowledge. Thus, being able to read proficiently and fluently is both powerful and empowering. As a child, I was warned numerous times about how nosy *I* was, because I read other people's letters, telephone messages, newspaper clippings, recipes, grocery lists, or anything that was left out on the kitchen counter, my mother's desk, or the family couch. I wasn't nosy, so that I could gossip or elevate my sense of superiority. However, it was quite true that I was unsatisfied with my life. I didn't want to butt in just so that I could find faults or bad news. I simply felt like I was constantly missing information being shared in the hearing world around me—the chatter among my parents, family members, and their friends that everyone present could hear but me. So, I discovered that the various items containing things to read served as useful clues for me. It didn't seem fair that my younger brother got to overhear things. I wanted to know who called, or what my dad wanted, or what we might be having for dinner one night.

I also read plenty of other material, including comic books, newspapers, and books, to satisfy my curiosity and thirst for knowledge. After reading dozens of easy children's picture books, I progressed to chapter books, particularly those about horses. At the time, my entire world was about horses. My mother owned a horse, and I rode some of the other horses in a stable. Although I read a few nonfiction books on taking care of and riding horses, I particularly treasured *Misty of Chincoteague* and other books written by Marguerite Henry. As it turned out, this author lived in Wayne, Illinois, where my father grew up. His family lived just down the lane from the author and had spent time with her and her numerous pets, including the horses who were the inspirations for her stories. I remember being surprised that the setting (on a coastal island) in *Misty* was not in Illinois after all. It intrigued me that an author could write about a place far away from home. This concept led to my interest in geography and maps, which I could pore over for hours. To this day, especially while traveling, I have an enduring curiosity as to what makes a town tick and why people live where they live.

When I was in fifth grade, I fell off a horse and suffered a serious fracture of my left humerus, the upper arm bone between my elbow and shoulder. I was out of school for a few weeks and spent much of the time in my parents' king-sized bed as I healed. The only color television in the house was placed at the foot of their bed, although it was of little use in entertaining me. Every few days, my neighbor or my brother would bring me some homework, usually simple sets of seatwork, such as anagrams, crossword puzzles, word searches, fill-in-the-blanks, and other word-level exercises that could be completed in a matter of minutes.

Because my friends were all in school, the days dragged on forever. I passed the time watching the ticking of minutes and seconds on my father's clock, taking plenty of naps, and reading books. My horse books had been well read, and I was tiring of them. So, I moved on to the beloved children's novels by E. B. White (*Stuart Little* and *Charlotte's Web*) along with those by Laura Ingalls Wilder (*Little House in the Big Woods* and *Little House on the Prairie*). I read *Charlie and the Chocolate Factory* and *James and the Giant Peach* by Roald Dahl. Not only did I enjoy riding horses, I loved messing about in boats and thoroughly enjoyed *Wind in the Willows* by Kenneth Grahame. When I was healed and back out and about, I delightfully discovered a whole new world around me—a world that was not all about horses after all.

Interestingly, although I have read many children's books, comic books were not really a part of my childhood. That is, until one very wet rainy weekend with my friend Amy and her family at their cottage up in northern Michigan. This was not a typical cottage in the middle of a thick pine forest; it was on a small island in the middle of a grand lake. The cottage was tiny, only one bedroom, set on an equally tiny island one tenth of an acre. There was no running water, so Amy's family brought in drinking water from the mainland. They boiled buckets of water from the lake to wash dishes. And yes, there was an outhouse. Propane in large tanks was brought over by motorboat for hooking up to the stove, refrigerator, and a few lamps on the walls. None of that mattered when it was warm and sunny, as we spent all of our time swimming and playing around in boats. However, the one weekend it rained, it poured for two whole miserable days.

On the island, we had absolutely nothing to do but play board games and read comic books. The treasure trove of comic books was kept in a large cardboard box and it entertained us for hours. Some of the comics portrayed *Richie Rich*, the child of incredibly wealthy parents, along with their butler. At first, I couldn't imagine anyone being richer than Amy's family; after all, they owned an island, albeit a wee one at that. I also remember reading about the entire *Peanuts* gang and the beloved dog, Snoopy. However, most of the comic books revolved around Archie, Betty, Veronica, and Jughead. Archie was a typical teenage boy caught in some sort of love triangle between Betty and Veronica. I was quite puzzled by this concept, as my perception of the opposite sex at that time was still in the cootie phase. I remember reading these comic books with studious interest, trying to figure out for the life of me what was going on between these characters or even if there was any kind of narration with a beginning, middle, and end like in a children's story.

* * *

Back in school, about once a week, everyone in my class had to bring in a current event article from our local newspaper to share with the class. Because each person had to stand up in front of the class and present the information from her or his chosen article, I would have only a faint idea of what they were talking about unless I had had a chance to glimpse the article, or at least the headline. Most of the time, I was not shown the newspaper clipping. I was always afraid of being accused of being nosy, so I would look for the articles at home. I always wondered what some of my classmates would find interesting enough to bring to school and share. My parents, however, made it a rule that my brother and I were not to start reading the newspaper until after they were finished with it. They didn't like the newspaper taken apart and scattered all over. But it seemed that the newspapers were never read, so I waited until they ended up in the garage.

Now, our two-car garage was not your typical garage. Back in the corner was a dark concrete stairwell that led to the lower level of our house. And this was where I spent quite a bit of time, sitting on the bottom step with the pile of boots and wooden crates of empty soda bottles, searching for the articles that my classmates had previously discussed in class.

Not only did I sit at the bottom of the garage stairwell steps, I have fond memories of making quick early morning jaunts to a village store in New Jersey and to the Blue Front in Ann Arbor with my Granddad to pick up the Sunday newspapers. At the Blue Front, newspapers in various languages were neatly stacked on a long platform along one wall, a lot like at a typical New York City newsstand. I remember being awfully curious, looking over the headlines, never touching the papers, trying to make sense of the Chinese characters and German words. At the same time, I was fully aware that the owner didn't like little children in his store. I knew that some children had been stealing some of the thousands of comic books in stock and attempting to catch a glimpse of the adult-only magazines, but I was only fascinated with the news-papers. I assumed that all of the headlines were the same, so if I read the top headline in the *The New York Times*, I thought I would be able to decipher the alphabets and words in the other newspapers. I walked back and forth, studying the papers until it was either time to leave or the owner finally got nervous enough to send me outside to wait for my grandfather.

* * *

Addison and I were both considered nosy children, but actually we were empowered through the world of text. Fortunately, we both outgrew our nosiness as we became proficient and fluent readers and entered into the world of books and other reading material. Literacy develops by reading short and easy material (such as notes or emails!), rereading familiar children's picture books over and over again, and reading books about a single topic (like horses!) for a long time. Finally, people move from *learning to read* to *reading to learn* about all kinds of topics. After all, reading *is* a socially sanctioned nosy activity!

THE GARGOYLES

IT IS SAID THAT a picture is worth a thousand words. Conversely, a picture often needs a thousand words to convey its meaning. It is one thing to see a picture, even with captions consisting of few words, but quite another to find out the connection and personal significance of it. What does the picture mean to the person who took it? Although a picture may stay in one's mind, words have staying power too.

Justin, who went by the nickname J. J., was a tall, physically fit tenth-grade student. He worked out by lifting weights, running, and playing basketball, tag, and soccer with his crowd of younger siblings, cousins, and neighbors. Even though he had a tough persona, he was a sweet and caring guy. Recently, J. J. had given up on the idea of being a star basketball player in college. Too many people—his teachers, his mentor, his coaches, and the principal—were on his case about doing better in school. J. J.'s mother was desperately trying to see to it that he finished high school. She knew the disturbing statistics about black teenage boys and the education system. She fretted that J. J. would drift from trouble to trouble, end up being suspended or incarcerated for even minor (or worse) infractions, or get wrongfully shot by the police. So, his mother made calls—many tearful and angry calls—to appeal for help. She called teachers, principals, coaches, mentors, their minister, and even the superintendent. And I was called.

It took some time for J. J. to trust me. The teaching profession in elementary through secondary schools is largely dominated by white women. I was yet another one. However, J. J. was intrigued that I was deaf. We started out having frank conversations about marginalization from a hearing black male versus a deaf white woman perspective. J. J. admitted that he hated school and wanted to drop out. I told J. J. about the time I played Cat and Mouse with a high school teacher, was set up to fail a class, and almost didn't graduate. J. J. said that he didn't feel like anyone cared about him before and asked why all the teachers and administrators were being called now on his behalf. He knew that his mother loved him deeply and wanted what was best for him, but he added that there was no way that he was going to be able to learn to read in time for graduation. So, we started to work together on his literacy. As it turned out, J. J. knew how to read. He got stuck only on longer words, like *forbidden, cardigan,* and *dilapidated.* Although J. J. knew these were long words that he needed to somehow decode, he said he couldn't "picture" them. He sounded them out a little bit, but then finally blurted out, "I don't know all these big white people words!" I sympathized with him and said, "Sometimes I don't either! I don't even hear them!"

* * *

The depth and breadth of a person's vocabulary, including the ability to picture words, is associated with literacy and is, of course, a huge focus in schools. Many adults can remember those dreaded vocabulary lessons in which they had to compare, classify, and analyze word roots, affixes, antonyms, and synonyms. However, when there are upwards of three-quarters of a million words in the English language, we can surely expect that no one individual knows all of them. Even the second edition of the 20-volume *Oxford English Dictionary* contains full entries for only 171,476 words in current use.

Deaf and hard of hearing children face considerable challenges in acquiring vocabulary appropriate for their ages. In fact, I'm always asked how I managed to acquire such a large vocabulary. The truth is that I didn't simply acquire it. Instead, I searched for it. However, looking up words was always the easy part. Making connections between a definition and the world around me was the challenging part. In a high school art class, the teacher wrote the word *gargoyles* on the chalkboard, so that I could read the word, but she didn't present any visual examples. She went on to describe a gargoyle as a human, bird, or animal face or figure, usually carved out of granite, projecting from the gutter of a building, with the throat and mouth typically acting as a medieval rainspout. Gargoyles were said to frighten off evil or harmful spirits and guard those inside, say, in a church. Of course, having never heard of this word and not being able to keep up with the teacher's description of it, I wrote the word down in my notebook and put yet another large question mark near it in the left margin.

We didn't have a textbook for this particular art class, so immediately upon arriving home, my curiosity having grown more intense throughout the rest of the day, I looked up *gargoyles* in my childhood dictionary. This was the dictionary originally given to me, so that I could learn how to pronounce words, using the symbols from the pronunciation key prominently placed on the inside of the front cover. Not surprisingly, the word was not in this particular dictionary, for I had largely outgrown it. So, I scrambled downstairs to our bookshelf in the family room to look up *gargoyles* in our set of encyclopedias. This was the same set of encyclopedias that I discovered at our neighborhood A&P grocery store while I was still in elementary school. Back then, grocery stores were solely for selling meat, dairy, and produce along with Campbell's Soup, Cheerios, and other brand name products, so I was tickled pink when I saw a table between the aisles and checkout lanes topped with volumes from a set of encyclopedias. Even though I knew not to touch, some of the volumes were open and I had to take a look. I immediately saw that it was like a dictionary but that the entries, in alphabetical order, were longer and more detailed. Some even had pictures! I remember pulling my harried mother, with a cart full of groceries and a whining little brother, over to see it and pleading with her to buy a set. Sure enough, *gargoyles* had an entry in our encyclopedia along with a picture. Finally, I had a visual image of gargoyles in my mind.

Once I found my nose in a dictionary or a particular volume of the encyclopedia, I would get distracted and start reading . . . and reading and reading. I spent hours sitting cross-legged on the floor reading one fascinating entry after another, yet the dictionaries and encyclopedias gave me straightforward definitions and concepts. They didn't always help me put things into context in my classes. I found out what gargoyles are, but I didn't know why the art teacher brought them up. What did gargoyles have to do with anything in my art class? I had to go back to school to find out that the topic had been artistic motifs, and the teacher had used gargoyles as an example of an architectural motif. She repeated the assignment to me, which was to include some kind of pattern or motif in our next project.

Today, more and more classroom and public presentations offer visual examples, such as slides or videos, but because they rarely have captions, I still miss information. At a public meeting for a local natural area, I was assured there would be a PowerPoint presentation to help me keep up with the speaker. However, I could see from the slides that *turtles* and *salamanders* were becoming increasingly endangered, but the biologist was actually talking about them in local terms. I had no idea that, even though they were becoming endangered nationwide, that there was actually a healthy population of salamanders in this particular park. I knew that some of the plants shown on the slides were invasive, but I wanted to know what the staff of this park was going to do about them or what I could do to be part of the volunteer efforts. That information never came.

It is not enough just to know words and their definitions. It is not enough just to see pictures either. We use some common words in our everyday lives, whereas other words are highly specific or infrequently used. There are words we barely recognize, because we've seen or heard of them only a few times before. We can understand and comprehend other words, but are not really able to use them appropriately. There are still other words that make us stop and wonder if we have ever heard or seen them before. Thus, we seek more information on the unknown words by asking, discussing, and even using search engines. And because language is ever evolving, new words regularly enter our lexicon, and old-fashioned words are hardly used anymore. Therefore, no one should view vocabulary and literacy as owned by the schools or even white people.

Although children may master nearly all of the features of their native language and can produce and understand most linguistic structures by the time they are four or five years of age, subsequent language development over a lifespan primarily involves increasing vocabulary. The real problem regarding limited vocabulary is not due to diminished brain capacity in an individual, but rather a lack of opportunity for partaking in a rich language and literacy environment. Researchers have found huge differences in the quantity and quality of the linguistic input that children receive, not only among deaf and hard of hearing children, but also among those who come from families with poorer economic means and those who learn English as a second language .

J. J. was not entirely off the mark when he declared that he didn't know "big white people words." He and his family were active participants in their community, culture, and language, but they were not part of the culture and language used in schools. J. J. and his mother valued education and knew that it was a ticket to economic success. And they knew that using "big white people words" was important in education and workplaces. However, from early on in kindergarten, J. J. was seen as having deficits in his ability to learn, and as a result, he received a different education than his white peers. Due to his covert segregation with other students like him, he never had robust opportunities to be exposed to and learn "white people words."

Children like J. J. are at risk for *linguistic overprotection*, which occurs when other people intentionally reduce, or water down, the linguistic complexity of their communication. This limits students' opportunities to learn more advanced language and concepts; for example, using *sick* instead of *infectious disease*. Although *linguistic overprotection* is a term used primarily in Deaf studies, it certainly applied to J. J. who could hear but was perceived as coming from an impoverished environment. As a result, J. J. suffered years of linguistic overprotection from "big white people words." In fact, when I assured J. J. and his teachers that he was a fine reader and that his brain was fully capable of learning new words over his lifespan, he gained the confidence to finish high school.

J. J. and I met once a week to develop strategies for learning words like *forbidden, cardigan,* and *dilapidated*. We worked on determining meaning from context, seeking definitions on his cellphone, and opening up and having discussions about new words. J. J. still called long words "big white people words" but with much more humor and willingness to grasp their meaning and significance.

When schools operate with the mind-set that vocabulary acquisition is a lifelong pursuit, it reduces the need for linguistic overprotection and special/separate classes. Children and adults, whether hearing or deaf, can enrich their vocabulary and language by listening, watching captions, and having well-qualified interpreters. Although vocabulary and language can support reading, it is also true that reading can expand vocabulary and language. And just as J. J. could learn "big white people words," I could learn some of the vocabulary and language used in his community and culture too.

SNAP, CRACKLE, POP

IN REGARDS TO THE *snap, crackle, pop* that is supposedly heard in a bowl of Rice Krispies, I wonder if these are three actually different sounds or if the words are simply three different ways to describe the one sound heard in that bowl of cereal. To me, all of the toasted rice grains in the bowl *look* identical. Furthermore, I don't even *see* them do any snapping, crackling, or popping. They just sit there in a pool of milk and turn to mush if I don't eat them up quickly.

Onomatopoeia is the formation of words whose pronunciation resembles the sound a thing makes, like *buzz* and *clang*. Reading onomatopoeia can even give a deaf person a clue as to what things sound like. Ethan, a second-grade child who told me his favorite cereal was Rice Krispies, was unwilling to wear his hearing aids most of the time. He was always getting into mischief and was not reading on grade level. His teacher told me that if he would just wear his hearing aids, especially during reading instruction, everything would be fine.

Many people don't realize that even the most sophisticated hearing aids are not a cure for hearing loss. In reality, aids amplify all sounds and do not always adequately discriminate the sounds of speech. Wearing hearing aids is not like putting on a pair of glasses and having one's vision corrected perfectly. This means that even while wearing his hearing aids, Ethan still needed to have his teacher face him, so he could lip-read her. He still needed tactile and visual supports for instruction, such as cueing, pointing, pictures, and even reading. Unfortunately, when Ethan had his hearing aids on, his teacher assumed he would function like his hearing peers. She thought Ethan didn't need extra assistance. Because this was an unrealistic assumption, Ethan increasingly refused to wear his hearing aids. Over time, he found that he had better support from adults and his peers when his hearing aids were left at home or hidden away in his locker.

Ellie preferred Cocoa Puffs. She, too, was delayed in her reading. A bright-eyed third-grader, Ellie wore a *cochlear implant*, which is a

173

device that is surgically embedded in the inner ear to provide electrical stimulation from the auditory nerve to the brain. Although people with cochlear implants are able to hear some speech and some environmental and musical sounds, the quality of sound is still different than natural hearing. Just like children who wear hearing aids, children with cochlear implants, like Ellie, still need varying accommodations, but all these children are fully capable of learning to read. Because Ellie had her surgery when she was six years old, she was undergoing aural rehabilitation, speech therapy, and learning to read all at the same time. It was definitely a lot for such a young child to handle.

Brent, also in third grade, liked Froot Loops. He wore hearing aids in both ears due to a severe to profound hearing loss. At his previous school, his teachers made sure he could read, which was, of course, a good thing. However, they made him read aloud to one of his teachers or an aide every day, not only for him to work on his reading, but also for him to practice his speech sounds. Brent told me they stopped him every time he missed certain sounds and that he then had to practice that word in isolation several times before going back and reading the text aloud again. When he arrived at my school and was put on my caseload, I found that Brent was so focused on his enunciation that he had absolutely no comprehension of any material I gave him.

And then there was Jennifer, a second-grader who was referred for special education. Jennifer's teachers assumed she had cognitive deficits, because she never seemed to understand directions, had a low repertoire of vocabulary words, and often seemed to have a deer-in-the-headlights look on her face. She wouldn't even tell me what kind of breakfast cereal she liked. Regardless, I noticed that Jennifer watched her peers carefully for cues for what she was supposed to do, such as get her coat on for recess, and was always well behaved. I also noticed that when I sat down on the floor in front of her, she watched my face closely and did much better learning to read in a quiet, one-on-one environment. After gently urging her parents to have Jennifer's hearing evaluated, it turned out she actually had a moderate hearing loss in both ears. And the tests she took for special education eligibility showed that her cognitive abilities were well within the normal range.

Although all these students liked different kinds of cereal, Ethan, Ellie, Brent, and Jennifer had diagnosed or undiagnosed hearing losses and were not reading "on time." All four of them were considered "at risk" by third grade, which is not all that unusual. Only one-third of our nation's fourth-graders, most of whom are hearing, read at or above the proficient level. Of course, standardized testing is a controversial issue, but the opportunity to learn to read is paramount and too often lost in our educational discussions and policies. Children in kindergarten are screened in beginning reading skills, and some are identified for intervention or special education when what they need is to have an adult read to them more and to carry on conversations about everything around them, help them learn the alphabet and explore the world of letters, sounds, and words. When they are removed from their peers and placed in resource rooms, they can have even fewer opportunities for rich language and literacy experiences.

Playing with letters, sounds, and words is one of the predictors of success in learning to read and write. In addition to onomatopoeia, certain letters and sounds pair up to spell related words. For example, Bryson noted there are a number of *sp*-words pertaining to wetness: *spray, splash, spit, sprinkle, splatter, spatter, spill*, and *spigot*. And a number of *fl*-words are associated movement: *flail, flap, flicker, flounce*, and *flee*. Words ending in *-ash* often describe abrupt actions: *flash, dash, crash, bash, thrash, smash*, and *slash*. Many children catch on to *alliteration*, the repetition of initial sounds; *assonance*, the repetition of vowel sounds; and *consonance*, the repetition of consonant sounds, by being surrounded with language, listening to amusing children's books, and plain goofing off with words. The point is not entirely about onomatopoeia itself, but about missed opportunities for developing language and literacies in an exuberant, vigorous, and authentic manner.

Despite the reality that I have never heard many sounds that can be found in onomatopoeia, I am literate. I can read. I can write. I can comprehend. I can summarize, analyze, synthesize, critique, and make connections. However, defining literacy directly depends on who defines it. Throughout my lifetime, I have been questioned about my literacies, because of the widespread assumption that deaf people do not read past a third- or fourth-grade level. Each time, I have been reminded of the political use of literacy tests, particularly in the southern United States. From the 1890s to the 1960s, many states required prospective voters to take a literacy test before they were deemed as competent to vote. The truth is that these tests deliberately disenfranchised racial minorities. Indeed, I am continually aware of the risks in confronting stereotypes and marginalization as I experience intense questioning, such as in the following incidences from my life, when my personal, professional, and academic literacies were questioned.

Because the percentage of deaf and hard of hearing children is relatively low compared to the general population, and therefore, in public schools, I don't often have these children on my caseloads. However, when children like Ethan, Ellie, Brent, and Jennifer come across my path, people's reaction to the idea of me working with them has always been extreme. On the one hand, some people think that I should not work with children who have a hearing loss, because I'm deaf and would not serve as a good model of language and literacy for them. On the other hand, some people think that I would be perfect to work with them, because I am deaf and would have empathy for them. However, the most common attitude that I face is that if I'm deaf, I should work only with deaf children in deaf schools, because I could not possibly work effectively with hearing children.

Once I was at my payroll office to address an error in my pay stub but was immediately told that I was at the wrong place. The accountant explained in a condescending manner that the district didn't hire teachers for the deaf. Although several classrooms for deaf children were housed in some of our district buildings, my district was not responsible for their fiscal operations. It took my identification badge for him to believe that I was indeed an employee within his district. When he saw that I worked as a teacher consultant, he immediately asked, "So... what are you reading then?" Thinking at first that I could not possibly be a reader, much less a teacher, he was satisfied when I shared various titles and synopses of the current books on my night stand. Suddenly, it seemed to me that getting the error on my paycheck rectified was going to be a challenge, one that depended on passing his informal literacy test. Not wanting to argue or appear indignant, I remained in good humor, calm, and professional, so as to avoid further microaggression and backlash. I was able to get the paycheck issue settled. If I were to call him out on his stereotyping, the onus would be on me to explain my inappropriate anger.

Indeed, my ability to work professionally as a teacher is frequently called into question. It's rare that I find myself in a debate with a student, but I once had an argument over a spelling word. Now I, of all people, should know better than to challenge anyone about any kind of word. Not only that, I should have remembered not to argue with a fifth-grader. This fifth-grader happened to be writing about her favorite kind of cheese. She was having difficulty spelling *Parmesan* and wanted my support. Of course, I wasn't going to tell her outright the correct spelling; I wanted her to practice using her tools to spell words on her own. So, we pulled out a small dry erase board and a first-generation hand-held spelling checker. (Nowadays, there are more sophisticated online spell checkers and auto-correction software.)

The student clapped out the number of syllables and tentatively wrote *par-ma-shon* on the dry erase board. Not thinking clearly that day, I insisted that it wouldn't work on her spelling checker, because *Parmesan* does not have a /sh/ sound in it. She vehemently insisted that it did contain the /sh/ sound while I, despite this nagging doubt in my head that maybe I'd been saying it wrong my whole life, insisted that it had sort of a /zh/ sound. We both began to look like squabbling little kids. Finally, she called over a speech and language therapist who happened to be passing by my office to ask how *Parmesan* is pronounced. Unfortunately, this speech and language therapist was as skeptical about my teaching literacy as the clerk at the payroll office. No matter, the fifth-grader learned that words are not always spelled the way they sound and are not always even pronounced the same way either. And I learned that some people in my area do pronounce *Parmesan* with a /sh/ sound. It must be one of those words with multiple pronunciations among people who can hear, but as a deaf professional, the standard was that I should have known better. The speech and language therapist immediately reported to the principal that I shouldn't be working with children in language and literacy, especially children who were in remedial or special education. Fortunately, this principal listened to my side of the story, and I was able to soldier on in my position.

Over the years, I also have been questioned about my academic literacy. Because I have a deep interest in literacy studies and am wary of studies that result in stereotyping populations, I keep abreast of new developments in literacy as well as education. Shortly after finishing my master's degree program, I applied to a doctoral program at the University of Michigan. I wanted to pursue an interdisciplinary degree between the departments of Early Childhood Education and Reading and Literacy. I wanted to focus on how young children, particularly those who are minorities, have disabilities, or have illiterate adult caregivers, develop language and literacies. At the time, the university was in the process of actively recruiting distinguished professors in the field of *emergent literacy*, a stage of early childhood development when a child moves from scribbling and reciting the ABCs to the stage of actually reading and writing. So, I thought this was a good fit and good timing for me. Unfortunately, upon finding out about my deafness early in the interview, the nationally known professor made it very clear to me that "deaf people cannot do sound research." She made a gesture signaling perfection made by connecting the thumb and forefinger to form a circle. The irony of her assertion was not lost on me. She used the word *sound* as an adjective, meaning to be *thorough*, *complete*, and *flawless*. I tried to set her straight that my deafness would not have any bearing on my ability to interpret, partake in, conduct, and write research studies. Because she worried about my inability to accurately hear children during the collection of raw data, I explained that data collection is only a small part of a research project. I also told her that, as a team, we could come up with creative ways to resolve this issue. Ultimately, though, I was not accepted. And at the time, I had no legal protections to pursue a discrimination complaint.

Defining literacy precedes testing, questioning, or challenging other people's literacies. Ethan, Ellie, Brent, Jennifer, and I each dealt with expectations that were unreasonable, namely that we needed the ability to *hear* in order to be literate. Reading, writing, and even spelling allowed me to access literacy, sounds, and even onomatopoeia. Reading and writing—and language and literacy—are interrelated and interconnected. Although many studies show that hearing children who play with letters and words learn to read and write more easily, deaf and hard of hearing children can learn to read, write, and play with letters and words in print as well.

Language and literacies do not always develop on the same timetable for *all* people. There are just too many pieces and puzzles in the constellation of what we call *language* and *literacy* to learn in a neat and packaged sequence, no matter what pediatricians, educators, politicians, and testing corporations may say. Furthermore, just because someone is missing a piece of language and literacy or has been the victim of miscommunication or ignorance, or is simply in a state of exploration about any feature of a language or literacy, does not mean he should be declared *globally illiterate* or *incompetent*. Instead, we are better for it when we can all embrace language and literacies on a rich and vibrant continuum.

THE ODYSSEY

CRITICAL THINKING and criticizing are two very different concepts. It's easy to criticize something or someone over a difference of opinion or to win arguments, but critical thinking involves a dedicated search for meaning and understanding. Developing the critical thinking, problem-solving, and analytical skills—and literacies—that are necessary in higher education, successful careers, political activism, and personal well-being can certainly feel like an epic journey. Critical thinking requires a person to *think* things through in a conscious and mindful manner.

Marshall, a stocky ninth-grader with black-rimmed glasses, asked his teacher with exasperation, "But why would you BUY a book?" He was genuinely surprised that some people actually buy books. He only knew of books in the school library or those issued as textbooks. Because these books were what many schools considered *safe literacy*, material that avoids controversial topics, Marshall declared them *sissy, bland,* or *boring.* Seriously, why would a person want to buy them?

Marshall came from a family whose parents bought children's books when he and his four siblings were younger, because they knew that reading aloud to children was an important start to their education. But this was the extent of their family literacy when it came to books. The family of seven could not afford to buy books on a tight budget. They also discovered early on that if they borrowed books from the public library, the books were prone to getting lost among all the children and subjected to replacement costs and hefty fees. Surely, Marshall would question why people would buy books; he didn't even remember his parents buying books.

The lack of books in Marshall's home, however, did not mean the family was illiterate or that they didn't value education. In fact, if Marshall hadn't brought up his question about buying books, no one at his school would have suspected that there were no books in their home. Marshall's parents helped with homework and encouraged their children to do well in school. They listened to the news online and had family discussions over dinner every evening. They all went shopping and enjoyed at least one outing on Saturdays, went to church on Sundays, and paid their bills every week. But theirs was a family who encouraged each other to question authority, challenge the status quo, and make themselves and their world a better place.

Marshall had walked into his English class a few minutes early and noticed his teacher, Ms. Russell, was engrossed in a paperback book while finishing up her lunch. Ms. Russell had barely noticed the time or Marshall's arrival in the classroom. Marshall watched her for a few minutes and fretted that the class was going to get "'nother stinkin' 'signment" that one of his classmates, Jamison, was always complaining about. No longer able to contain his curiosity, Marshall strolled up to Ms. Russell's desk and asked if the book she was reading was going to be their next assignment. Ms. Russell looked up and remarked, "Oh no, this is a book I bought yesterday, and I'm thoroughly enjoying reading it on my lunch break." Marshall's exasperated question about buying books gave her pause.

Instead of beginning the English class as she had planned, Ms. Russell, with my support as a literacy consultant, decided to open a discussion about buying books and reading for pleasure. As she listened carefully, many of her students said that teachers at the school assumed that they couldn't read well. They admitted to not liking the material that they were required to read, especially when some of the topics didn't make sense, were unrelatable, or were boring. And a few students mentioned they were even offended by the choices of books the teachers made, because the material seemed "babyish." They admitted to not reading novels assigned by their teachers, because only a few of their classmates, those who were called the *smart ones*, would find it interesting enough to actually read it. The rest of the class would just wait to hear about the chapters at each discussion. They chorused loudly that their social studies, health, and science textbooks were depressingly clunky to get through. Jamison even blurted out that they just contained "one stinkin' fact after another," and none of it was even interesting. When Ms. Russell asked about the school library, the students groaned that the books were old, dirty, and out of date. The clothing and hairstyles on the covers of the library books were two decades old.

After Ms. Russell fully listened to Marshall and her students, she realized that they were unengaged, unempowered, and apathetic. She came to see that the problem was not their perceived deficits as at-risk students but rather was the school's problem. She took a few moments after school to review the holdings in the library and was appalled. The librarian, who was in the building only one hour a week, had not ordered new books in more than ten years because of education budget cuts. Schools in poorer areas have fewer outside resources for the very reasons that the community—the parent donors, the local grantors, and the struggling businesses—has limited funds to support the schools. Ms. Russell fretted about the state of the library and about assigning a single novel to her entire class. She wanted Marshall and all of her students to experience the same pleasures of reading that she did during her lunch hour. She realized that if her students were not reading at home and they were not reading at school, they were simply not reading.

I can still recall the novels assigned for my various English classes. We would read two or three books, such as *The Great Gatsby, Grapes of Wrath, Macbeth, Fahrenheit 451, The Old Man and the Sea, A Tale of Two Cities, One Flew Over the Cuckoo's Nest, Uncle Tom's Cabin,* and *The Odyssey,* over the entire course of a semester. Of course, I remember some of my peers complaining about having to read these required books, and a few of them read Spark Notes or didn't read them at all. However, from my little bubbled world, it seemed to me that most of the discussions during my classes were animated and even high-spirited at times, discussions that I could see going on but was not a part of. Although I liked reading most of these books, my first and foremost concern was passing the tests.

As I've mentioned, I relied on my classmates' notes during high school. I struggled to keep up with the teachers' lectures and classroom discussions after reading assigned chapters. Each evening, armed with my own notes and two of my friends' notes, I put the pieces of the puzzle together in an orderly and comprehensible manner and rewrote all of the notes in my own notebook. It was not long before I discovered that two people could hear the same thing in class but come away with differing interpretations of what they heard. This really struck me as odd, for I thought everyone could hear the same way. Wasn't that the whole purpose of having a teacher stand in the front of the class and lecture on a topic or another?

In one literature class, we read a translation of *The Odyssey*. Odysseus took ten long adventurous years to reach his home in Ithaca after the ten-year Trojan War. Because of his twenty-year absence, most of his countrymen assumed that he had died. While Odysseus was gone, his wife, Penelope, and son, Telemachus, had to fend off a large group of unruly suitors who competed for Penelope's hand in marriage. *The Odyssey* contains multiple themes, including homecoming and the triumph of cleverness and disguise over strength, temptation, and hospitality. However, in reviewing the notes, one wrote that the primary theme of *The Odyssey* was homecoming, and the other wrote that it was cleverness and disguise. Who to believe? So, I had to do my research and determine for myself what the major theme was. Alas, all of these themes appeared to be relevant, but one didn't seem more *major* than another. What did the teacher *really* say? And more than that, was it going to be on the test? At the time, I wanted the right answer. It may have come across to other people as immaturity on my part, but I had not realized the extent of multiple perspectives or the diversity of opinions among my classroom peers. I was too focused on lipreading the teacher and making sense of my collection of notes.

When I went to college, I quickly learned there were no *right* answers. The professors required essays, critiques, research papers, and thoughtful answers to open-ended questions. When I arrived for my first English class in college, I found that our required readings were the books I had already read in my progressive high school. This gave me a delightful opportunity to reread these books more deeply and to think about what they meant to me personally. It was also then that I had a strong desire to be *nosy* again and read my peers' essays, critiques, and papers, to see what they had to say about things. Of course, this wasn't possible, so I became an insatiable reader on all kinds of books, articles, and opinion pieces. Nowadays, I'm delighted with the proliferation of creative nonfiction books now available that use different literary styles and techniques to create narratives and memoirs, all of which expose me to a wider set of life experiences and worldviews.

Marshall, his peers, and I lacked opportunities for developing a broader sense of literacies. Marshall and his classmates were victims not only of poor resources, but also pressure from parents, community members, and the school administration to conform to safe and neutral ideas, despite the fact that some of them already had adult experiences too early in their lives. One reason that public schools avoid teaching critical thinking is that it necessarily involves controversies. Perhaps it is easier to legislate what constitutes virtue and character, but expectations for conformity can come at a cost when there is little encouragement to challenge authorities or even examine the relationships among them. Marshall challenged his teacher as to why people would want to buy books. Ms. Russell took up the challenge to listen to her students' points of view. Instead of maintaining the status quo, Marshal, his teacher, and classmates took a hard look at the disparaging situation in their school and worked to improve the library's collection by increasing awareness and seeking funds.

Critical conversations, even in schools, should get people thinking seriously about an important moral and/or political issue and to convince everyone that they are included as members in a participatory democracy. People need to be encouraged to raise challenging questions, navigate their way through complex issues, and still know how to retain their own cultural identity and belief systems. Even though I read a wide range of books considered controversial, confronted notes of differing perspectives, and saw there were high-spirited discussions in my classes, I was actually functioning in a concrete world, where I was only concerned about surviving school and getting good grades. I didn't question or think critically about social or political issues that came my way. In other words, I was simply a good girl.

Of course, reading and writing skills can be taught through bland texts, but it became obvious to Ms. Russell that the content of the material is the hook, the motivator, and source of empowerment. Furthermore, reading and writing skills, literacies, and a person's level of education are by far not interchangeable. In schools where there is much diversity, children and their families are too often viewed through their deficits and dilemmas rather than the richness of their heritages and experiences. Instead, consciously removing deficit mind-sets allows everyone to listen to, share, and respect all lives and life experiences. Marshall, his peers, and Ms. Russell, along with Ms. Russell's teaching team, began their odyssey toward reenergizing the English program by seeking funds and developing a workshop model in which all the students, whether singly, in pairs, or in small groups, chose a current and relevant title to read and discuss based on their worldviews. They practiced emotionally safe ways to express and learn about multiple cultural identities and belief systems. As for me, I was able to "listen" in on their spirited conversations through the use of real-time captioning by an expert stenographer, which allowed me to participate in a way I had never experienced when I was young.

PART 8

LINGUISTICS

INTRODUCTION: DEFINING LINGUISTICS

"Curiouser and curiouser!" cried Alice (she was so much surprised,
that for the moment she quite forgot how to speak good English).
                                                    —LEWIS CARROLL

LINGUISTICS IS THE SCIENTIFIC study of the nature and structure of language and languages. Linguistics claims to be a field of neutrality and objectivity, but of course, science, especially the social sciences, is not always objective. It is difficult to not be influenced by experiences, perspectives, values, biases, and emotional involvement, particularly with regard to sociolinguistics. *Sociolinguistics* is the study of the role of language in society; that is, the effects of politics, social class, economic power, religion, dialects, or gender, have on how we use language and are perceived by others. Deaf and hard of hearing people, people with speech and language disorders, and second language learners are aware of how their own speech and languages are similar to or different than that of the others around them. And they know all too well the effects of linguistic marginalization, in addition to or even without racial- or class-based inequities. When all of us foster curiosity, learn about, and acknowledge the personal and societal advantages some linguistic groups have over others, we can promote sociolinguistic justice in our classrooms, workplaces, and communities.

SPEAK ENGLISH

AT ONE TIME OR another, all of us have seen kids having a tantrum with both hands tightly clasped over their ears and their eyes shut, making it clear that they are not going to listen. Of course, the reason some people are not good listeners is because they simply won't listen. Dion, a friendly child with a delightfully comedic sense of humor and a sly grin to match was in fourth grade; but according to his teacher, he was still not reading. Because he was prone to mild outbursts with adults and sometimes got himself into tussles with other children, the administrators were concerned about him. They asked me to take him on, because they felt that he was frustrated with his reading and the increasing demands of the fourth-grade curriculum.

"I don't like you. I know you can't hear, and you talk funny," Dion told me the moment we met. I answered that I was far from perfect, and I asked him if he was perfect. Oh yes, he was perfect. So, with an agreeable smile, I mentioned that we should get started with reading. Dion shrunk in his chair and declared that he could not read, wouldn't read, and that he hated reading. With feigned puzzlement, I remarked, "But I thought you said you were perfect?" We had a gentle conversation about how no one is perfect, not even him. Not even parents, teachers, and principals, and especially not me, who can't even hear or talk right. I went on to explain that even though I was deaf and spoke differently, I was a good reader and could teach him how to read better too.

The next few days were not about perfection but about being scared. I saw that Dion was afraid to take risks. He knew he was far behind his peers in his classroom. While reading, Dion wanted me to tell him the words he got stuck on, a practice that perhaps for years, he was probably used to. And he wanted these words written on flash cards, so that he could practice memorizing them. I refused to do both, telling him words and writing them on index cards. Instead, I set to work demonstrating some cueing strategies, including phonics, so that he could figure out unknown words on his own. However, with each unsuccessful attempt at decoding an unknown word, Dion got terribly frustrated, slammed the book down, and went to pout by the door. There were times he even threw his chair and stormed out. I recognized these outbursts as frustration, not as oppositional behavior, so I sat and waited until he, on his own, returned to try again.

I saw that Dion had a strong desire to be able to read in a proficient and fluent manner. And he started to see that I was not going to send him to the office for his misbehavior. Neither of us gave up, and slowly, he began to trust me. It was not long before Dion revealed that if he didn't read something perfectly the first time, he would get called out on it by an adult. When I asked him to explain more, the entire story of his struggles with reading poured out. His mother worked a lot, especially at night—she had two jobs. His grandmother was the one who insisted on listening to him read every evening. She expected him to read out loud, sounding out words one by one correctly before moving on to the next word. Dion further complained that he was stuck on "baby books," because he could read them accurately.

If Dion got in trouble at school, which was often, the school called his uncle. From there, his uncle would tell his grandmother, and then his grandmother would make him "read double"—twice as many books—word by word with each uttered correctly. Dion felt that he was constantly being picked on. And not only that, according to what his grandmother told him, my way of teaching him how to read was wrong. He further remarked that his grandmother said that because she heard that I was deaf and spoke differently, he didn't have to listen to me either.

Here was a clash of assumptions and a lack of communication among the adults surrounding Dion's literacy instruction. When I shared this conversation with Dion's classroom teacher, she was surprised that there was any reading at all going on in his home. Dion was part of what educators consider a *traditionally underperforming* population group, in that he was black and lived in an impoverished home. Therefore, Dion's teacher did not expect that he was reading at home with his family; she had not realized the level of care his mother, uncle, and grandmother took to see that Dion learned to read and do well in school. Dion and his family had plenty of language and literacy practices in their home, including, but not limited to, reading books aloud, writing thank-you notes, talking about words and what they mean, and discussing the importance of school. But this was all cast aside as Dion and his grandmother focused on sounding out words and memorizing words on flash cards, because they worried that his teachers at school were not teaching him to read.

Dion's teacher had no idea that an aide was previously sending flashcards home with Dion for him to practice memorizing. The teacher had entrusted the aide, one who had no expertise in reading instruction, to work with him out in the hallway. And I had no idea either. Meanwhile, when I met his grandmother, she explained that the teachers at the school kept telling the family that they needed to help Dion read at home. The family worried that his teachers were not teaching him to read at school. She also explained that because they spoke black English, she wanted him to sound out and learn to read every word correctly in books. And yes, she said that she heard about deaf people typically reading at a fourth-grade level and was distressed to find out that her grandson was being taught to read by a deaf person.

Of course, there were feelings of tension, anger, and hurt among all of us. However, all of the adults around Dion agreed in a meeting that reading proficiently and fluently in our society is a crucial means toward educational and economic success. Starting with that agreement, we began the painful, but successful, process of repairing our assumptions and misunderstandings for Dion's future stake in his school career. I explained that even though I was deaf, literacy was my strongest skill. Literacy was a source of access to communication and learning new information for me. I also had expertise in emergent and developing literacy processes, particularly in children with diverse needs. The classroom teacher and the aide, with sorrow and embarrassment, acknowledged their ignorance and stereotyping of the family. The grandmother learned that since phonemes of syntax of spoken languages do not always match words in print, it was not necessary to read every word exactly for comprehension. And the uncle realized that tying literacy to punishment was probably not a good idea. These kinds of conversations to address diversity, differences, and disparity are difficult. Unfortunately, relationships can end quickly when people decide that they do not need to listen to one another.

And sometimes people are told to "get the hell out." Literally. Klaus, my husband, loves to bicycle and even repair and rebuild bikes. A friend, Pat, who was living in an apartment complex at the time, read in a distributed flyer that all of the bikes lying around were going to get rounded up if they were not claimed by a specific date. Klaus, Pat, and I went behind the dumpster, where dozens of bikes were placed after the date of the roundup. Klaus wanted to fix the smaller bikes to give to several friends' children. We were not the only ones behind the dumpster. There were two burly metal scrappers picking up old furnaces, saying that they could get $150 for each. Klaus and Pat struck up a friendly conversation with the men.

After the metal scrappers had loaded up their pickup truck and slammed the tailgate, I saw the bumper sticker: "God Bless America: Speak English or Get the Hell Out." Both men had moustaches and long, scraggly beards, so I couldn't lipread or keep up with the chatter. I was relieved that I hadn't said a word. I froze in place for a moment, double-checking the reality of this bumper sticker, one that I had never seen before. Then I retreated slowly, stepping backwards, like people should do if they confront bears in the woods.

I have been told numerous times to get the hell out within the first moments I say something. The first time was more than thirty years ago, when I worked as a newly hired early childhood educator for a Head Start program. I was making a required home visit as part of my professional duties in order to develop trusting relationships with families and offer parenting resources. The parents and their three children welcomed me inside. They had spent the morning tidying up their apartment, making lemonade, changing into clean clothes, and eagerly looking forward to their teacher's visit. The moment I sat down on their sofa, I found myself greeted by a cross grandfather, who yelled at me to leave his house immediately. He angrily pointed his finger toward the door. The children began to cry. The father quietly led me by the elbow back outside. Puzzled and shaken by the grandfather's outburst, I returned to my school, where my principal was waiting for me. The father had called ahead to explain that although I was pleasant during the exchange of greetings, I talked differently. The grandfather was upset that I didn't speak *properly* like a teacher should. He went so far as to insist that I should be fired. Fortunately, much to my relief, my principal supported me and refused to consider firing me.

I not only must contend with parents or guardians who are understandably concerned about their children's education, but also I have to deal with community members who are concerned about the quality of our school systems. During a wedding reception on the East Coast, I happened upon a discussion about the multiple languages children bring to our nation's schools. A high school teacher, just starting her career, was bemoaning the "poor English" (her words) spoken in her urban classroom in New York City. A business owner said she was worried about the number of children speaking Arabic in her community in southeast Michigan. While I was sharing my opinion that it was crucial for educators to acknowledge, and even embrace, the depth and breadth of our nation's linguistic diversity, a distinguished-looking older gentleman tapped my shoulder to warn me that he was a member of a school board in a small town in Pennsylvania. He had overheard, erroneously, that I was "teaching Ebonics or whatever language my accent came from," and he made it clear that he intended to report me to the school board in the school district where I worked. His position was that children must be taught only in English or they would not be able to pursue educational or economic opportunities in our country.

I tried in vain to explain that I was not teaching any languages or English language variations, but that it was crucial to help students, like Dion and his grandmother, see similarities and differences—and make connections—from their first language to the forms of English found in print in order to support their reading and writing skills. Unfortunately, the situation became worse. The man was particularly bothered by the way I spoke. He didn't believe that I was deaf, because I was somehow carrying on a conversation with him and others in the wedding reception. In the end, however, I never did hear a word from my district's school board. I have always walked a fine line between having to size up situations I am in with wariness versus being approachable, warm, and friendly, deaf accent and all.

I am in awe at the number of times I've been told to get the hell out or that I should be fired because of the way I speak. And I am equally in awe—and thankful—that my administrators over my career have stood by me and trusted me to work with the children in our district. Perhaps it helped that our small university town is rich with diversity; but, more than that, our strong leadership remains steadfast in promoting tolerance. Many people approach me with skepticism, and some are quick to express loudly their doubts of my capabilities as a reader, writer, learner, and educator. Even though manifestly unfair, people judge a speaker's intelligence, character, and personal worth on the basis of his or her spoken language. We ought to be aware of the power of such social stereotyping. Our languages—our accents, intonations, stresses, syntax, and semantics—create a first impression of who we are.

Although language and literacies are closely tied to ethnic, cultural, and linguistic identities, our accents, both foreign and regional accents as well as those due to speaking differently, are not changed easily. People are born capable of producing and perceiving all of the sounds of all human languages. In infancy, however, a child begins to learn what sounds are important in the surrounding language and to disregard the rest. The older one gets, the harder it becomes to learn the sounds that are part of a different language. Speech and language therapists are committed to helping children and adults with speech, language, and hearing disorders communicate effectively. But many speakers do not need a cure. Everett states that "language gets the job done just well enough, never perfectly." The reality is that *all* speakers, regardless of their languages, have an accent. From a linguistic standpoint, no one accent is superior to another. Such judgments about which accents are acceptable or unacceptable are entrenched within historical, social, and political contexts. Therefore, most people would be able to understand each other better, if they would just listen.

THE ANN ARBOR DECISION

APPARENTLY, SIRI, a virtual assistant in the artificial-intelligence world, does not listen well. Classmates Deja, Blake, Owen, and Markus were sitting together at a small round table in their English class, bathed in bright sunlight streaming in from the large windows. This was a supplementary English class for students on a high school diploma track who were not quite ready for other classes, such as Composition, Creative Writing, Argumentation, Journalism, or American, British, Women's, or African-American Literature. The students in this class were special education students, English language learners, or those who otherwise scored below target on achievement tests.

On the day I came to observe Deja, at the request of her parents and administration, the teacher, Mr. Jenkins, had rolled in a cart full of brand-new tablet computers. Mr. Jenkins enthusiastically explained that the speech-to-text software on the tablets could be used to assist with writing assignments. He showed the students how to open a new document and click on an icon showing a pencil. When the keyboard popped up, they could click on an icon showing a microphone. From there, the tablet would automatically type while a person was dictating. Mr. Jenkins demonstrated a few sentences, enunciating slowly and clearly: "Today is a beautiful sunny day. Wish today was Saturday. But this thing has an awesome app. You all try it now."

While two students passed out tablets from the cart, Mr. Jenkins found an online timer, projected it on the whiteboard, started the countdown, and invited the students to explore the speech-to-text software on their tablets for twenty minutes. I was baffled as to how an entire class of about twenty students would be able to talk into their individual tablets and get individual results. Wouldn't all the chatter of their dictations interfere with the automatically typed responses on their documents? A few students got up to move to new seats, but, to my surprise, most seemed to be working fine. However, at Deja's table near the corner by the windows, I saw Deja, Blake, Owen, and Markus laughing uproariously over their tablets. They were sharing the wacky outcomes of their dictation, some of which was somehow turned into Japanese or Greek characters. Being curious, I moved over to join them.

Deja, while able to switch between speaking more mainstream forms of English and African-American English, spoke African-American English into her tablet with futile results. Owen had a severe hearing loss, and Blake was recovering from a traumatic brain injury, so their speech was not accurately recognizable by the software on their tablets. Markus was able to make his speech work with the software, but then he started imitating Donald Duck and other cartoon characters with silly results. Although they found it all amusing, Blake and Owen quickly realized that speech-to-text software would be of no use to them for writing assignments. Deja discovered that if she spoke "proper English" (her words), her dictation worked better. Markus, on the other hand, voiced his concern about the inequity of this software. Only "perfect people" (his words), not his friends, could use the software. Because Markus aspired to be a computer engineer, he immediately started researching websites on the tablet and brainstorming how he would improve speech-to-text software, so that "everyone, including Donald Duck," could use it. Of course, Markus was discovering the complexity of computational linguistics.

Although speech recognition technologies have become more sophisticated and vastly improved since that day in the English class, they, like Siri, are still not the best of listeners. Mr. Jenkins insisted that speech recognition software was not meant to be accurate in the first place. He insisted that it was just a resource to help with writing assignments. He would teach them how to go back over their essays and edit for complete sentences, punctuation, and spelling. But Mr. Jenkins would not acknowledge that it didn't work *at all* for Blake and Owen. I could not use it either. Once I tried to use dictation on my smartphone to practice my own pronunciation. Not a single word came out right. I became so frustrated and embarrassed by my speech patterns that I fell to tears, and to this day, I refuse to try it again. Auto-generated captions on news media and in YouTube videos featuring hearing people rarely work well either. Real-time captioning by pairs of real ears is currently the most effective resource I have for watching television or listening to groups of people.

Blake and Owen needed to hear from Mr. Jenkins that he was willing to help them research and seek other resources to support their writing, such as word prediction software, spelling and grammar checks on word processors, and online dictionaries. Through Mr. Jenkin's lack of acceptance of their predicament with the speech recognition software, they felt marginalized, a situation that Markus was moved to change in his classroom. Markus began with acknowledging the unfairness of the speech-to-text software for Blake and Owen. Acknowledgment is the key word in beginning conversations about diversity and linguistics. What heartened me was how objective Deja, Owen, Blake, and Markus were in their dialogue about their various forms of languages, accents, speech disorders, and technology. As they were exploring the linguistics around them, they were supportive of each other with grace and much humor. Nelson Mandela said that "no one is born hating another person . . . they must learn to hate, and if they can learn to hate, they can be taught to love." There was much to love at this table.

I came of age at the tail end of the Great Migration of people of color from the South and during the lengthy and intense controversy surrounding the U.S. district court case of *Martin Luther King Junior Elementary School Children v. Ann Arbor School District* (also referred as the *Ann Arbor Decision*). The school district, involving a school just on the other side of Green Road from where I grew up, was sued for failing to consider that the children's use of black English in the home prevented them from making progress in reading. In 1979, the court ruled that the school district had to train teachers to identify the children who spoke black English and to teach them how to read and write in the standard English used in the school.

The neighborhood where I spent my childhood was filled with young professionals with families, professionals who worked at thriving pharmaceutical companies, the "Big Three" auto companies, in budding businesses, or on emerging technologies. There was a swimming pool, wooded natural areas, numerous courts to bike around in, and a large pond for exploring in the summers and ice skating in the winters. I can remember clearly, as if it were yesterday, a day when I was about six or seven years old, my father warned me to "be very nice" to the new "negro" family, with a little girl my own age, who was moving in down the street. But I was puzzled by my father's admonishment because my inner voice said, "*I* am different, and *I* want people to be nice to me." Absolutely, I would try to be nice to everyone, even to the new family down the street. Sometimes I came across as not being nice, because I would ignore people I didn't hear, but I always *tried* to be nice.

Of course, I played with the girl down the road. I wanted friends just as much as the new girl wanted friends, too. At the time, I had no idea about the shifts in American culture, society, and politics of the late sixties and early seventies, particularly with regard to desegregation and mainstreaming in schools. However, one of my vivid childhood memories is my confusion over the general disdain among the members of my community toward the spoken language of the families who lived on the other side of Green Road. My neighbors' attitude about black English puzzled me, because we had international children in my own school. These students came to Michigan because they had a parent who was a doctoral student or fellow at the university. They spoke with accents and varying levels of fluency in English, but I don't recall anyone making derogatory comments about the way *they* talked.

Being sensitive about the way I talk, I remember asking several adults around me why my neighbors were so upset by the black English spoken over on Green Road. After all, we did have nearby neighbors who were black too, and it seemed to me that we got along fine. Each time I brought the subject up, I was sharply rebuked and told that the issue of how people talk was different for me, simply because I don't hear. I was told that black people *can* hear, so they "should know better" and speak "correctly." With arms crossed or frowns, the adults made it clear to me that that was the end of the discussion. Looking back now, I understand that the issue of race, language, and cultural assimilation may have been an uncomfortable topic for adults to discuss with children. Still it didn't make any sense to me, because if the students and their families from abroad could also hear, shouldn't they know better, too? I honestly started to think that people could easily change the way they talked simply because they could hear. After all, most people who talked to me did try to speak a bit more slowly and clearly.

As much as I desired to have friends of all kinds, I began to think that people who didn't change their accents were not nice to me, or that they didn't want to be around or play with me. It was not until I met Aase, a girl from Norway who persistently tried to befriend me in ninth grade, that I started to think otherwise. Although Aase had a good grasp of English, she did have quite the accent when she arrived with her family. Aase and I made a sincere effort to communicate; she tried to lessen her accent and I tried to understand her. With time, we got used to each other and became close friends. We were even pen pals for more than a decade until I lost track of her, later finding out that she had died. Aase and I had classes together. We both loved walking and exploring, and we talked and talked. Aase and I dealt with our communication glitches with humor and grace, sparking my lifelong curiosity about language, literacy, and linguistics.

People who are linguistically different in any community are fully aware of it, whereas people who are part of the dominant language and culture do not give much thought to the characteristics of their own language until they learn a second language, take grammar courses, or are confronted with the language and linguistics of people unlike them. In her book, *Making All the Difference*, Martha Minnow compares judicial cases of inclusion, exclusion, and American law with the children's television show *Sesame Street*. Using animation, skits, and songs, the show asks, "Which one of these things is not like the others?" by showing a group of items, perhaps a chair, a table, a cat, and a bed. The intention is to help children expand their vocabulary, sharpen their perception, and analyze objects in our world. However, Minnow points out that when we identify one thing as like the others, we are not merely classifying the world, we are investing particular classifications with consequences and placing our views in relation to those meanings. When we identify one thing as unlike the others, we are dividing the world around us. We use our language to distinguish, to exclude, and to discriminate.

Deja, Blake, and Owen were unlike their peers in their high school. I am seen as unlike the others in a field of educators. On the basis of our speech and language and the associated stereotypes, we are, in turn, susceptible to discrimination throughout our entire lifetimes of educational, economic, professional, and recreational pursuits. Minnow points out in a compelling footnote that we can find similarities as well as differences; for example, the chair, table, cat, and bed each have four legs. Likewise, Deja, Blake, Owen, and I could be seen as fully capable readers, writers, learners, and educators—as viable and contributing members of our communities, no matter what language or language disorder we started our lives with. When we strive toward full inclusion, we hone our ability to teach all children, not just a select few. Inclusion can be compatible with high levels of achievement. In fact, combining the two is essential if *all* children are to have opportunities to partake fully in education.

Deja was on my radar as a student who was underachieving in school. Her parents and the administration were concerned about her lack of progress. However, the mind-set of *proper English* and *perfect people* was what needed to be removed; Deja's inherent capabilities for learning were not the issue. The lesson on learning how to use speech-to-text software, the lack of acknowledgment from Mr. Jenkins, and Markus's insistence on the unfairness of it all was a turning point for Deja. When she began to see herself, and others around her, as exploring language, literacies, and linguistics as someone without an intellectual or biological problem, her confidence to tackle challenging material grew. It was also a turning point for Blake and Owen. Too often, people with disabilities view themselves from a medical perspective, because that is how others see them. However, they can also consider themselves to be part of a cultural and/or linguistic minority. Open and tempered discussions can go a long way toward nurturing acceptance of our differences. The important thing to remember is that we are all human, worthy of opportunities to explore, learn, grow, belong, care, and love.

PART 9

CONCLUSION

KERFUFFLES AND KNICKERS
IN A KNOT!

THE CATCHPHRASE "the rich get richer and the poor get poorer" can be true when discussing economic and even educational outcomes. Some people say that trickle-down economics, in which the wealthy pass down benefits to everyone else, doesn't work too well. However, the successes of people with disabilities can lead to successes of other people with disabilities.

Trenton, a gifted childhood friend, who is hearing, grew up to be a researcher and professor of medicine. He wrote to me that growing up with me had an influence on the career of a young deaf woman working in his lab. Unfortunately, he had to wrangle with the university to provide a sign language interpreter for her. Throughout his advocacy process, Trenton was distressed that so many people asked him why he didn't just hire someone else. What a kerfuffle. Ultimately, Trenton reported that this woman's presence in their workplace was the best thing that happened to the group. They slowed down and became more mindful and clear about what they were communicating, and everyone even learned a bit of sign language. Because the woman and her ASL interpreter needed to preview material ahead of meetings, Trenton's staff was also succinct and better prepared. In essence, the woman taught Trenton's lab group much more about language, literacy, and communication. Trenton noted a profound difference in the quality, not just the quantity, of their experiences and work results.

At another university, Lee, a professor and chair in family medicine had a medical student apply to the residency program. The student was deaf, had good lipreading skills, and needed an interpreter for large meetings and case conferences. Such meetings occurred just once a week or so, but according to Lee, the hospital had their "knickers in a knot" over the idea of a deaf person in their midst. Although Lee knew at least three successful deaf professionals, the hospital staff had never dealt with deafness before, harbored all kinds of fears, and put up barriers to her residency. He was able to debunk many of their misconceptions about deafness, but the last sticking point involved money, for the hospital was reluctant to pay for sign language interpreters. Thankfully, Lee successfully made it clear that accommodations for disabilities are required by law, and the resident was able to join the staff and contribute to her profession.

Katie, a school nurse, and her sister, Lynn, a high school health science teacher, advocated for two deaf high school students who wanted to continue their education in public health. The adults, teachers, counselors, and administrators around them were skeptical about the students' capabilities as healthcare providers. One went so far as to exclaim, "If I were a patient, I wouldn't want a deaf person caring for me! That's dangerous!" Others wondered how the students could become nurses or doctors if they weren't able to discuss health care with their patients, use stethoscopes, or hear all the beeping machines. However, Katie and Lynn knew that there were accommodations for communication, visual or amplified stethoscopes, and significant advances in medical technology. They also knew that physician–patient relationships are crucial and that their two students carried life experiences, knowledge, strength, and empathy their patients would appreciate. One of the students brought three languages—American Sign Language, Arabic, and English—to her skill set. The other went on to copublish peer-reviewed papers for the American Medical Association. Both former students made Katie and Lynn proud as they continued to pursue their postsecondary education.

Trenton, Lee, Katie, and Lynn were hearing professionals in instructional, supervisory, or administrative positions, who advocated for young deaf people based on their strengths. They called upon their own steadfastness and confidence that their employees, residents, or students *could* and *would* succeed. I intimately know the world of brouhahas over my deafness. When a professor announced that I had the highest score of my graduating class on a secured state test required for a teaching certificate, I was loudly condemned by a classmate as a "cheater" in front of the entire class. When I was hired for a position in a public school, I was told that it was because "there was a special quota for people like me" and that it was "unfair," especially because I was "obviously unqual-ified for the job." During a meeting, a classroom teacher was irate about me being one of her students' case managers. She spewed forth many uncharitable reasons why a deaf person like me could not collaborate with her, not realizing her entire tirade was captioned for me to read. Almost always, I needed to hold my ground by remaining stoic and silent, but the moment I sat in my car to drive home, I would burst into hot tears of humiliation, rejection, and frustration. And almost always, the next day, I would pull myself together, put my chin up, and get back out there without telling anyone a word about the personal attacks against me for fear of backlash.

I am able to advocate for myself only some of the time; but in par-ticularly trying circumstances, I need my hearing peers and superiors to intervene before my predicaments are resolved. The *bystander effect*, which usually occurs during medical or mental emergencies or when there is bullying or other aggressive behaviors, comes into play when bystanders do nothing but watch or choose to stay out of the situation. Although bystanders may be uncomfortable and not know what to do, they unintentionally become part of the problem by allowing privilege, stereotypes, marginalization, microaggression, and hostility to continue.

Kerfuffle and knotted knickers arrived in my email inboxes, on my Facebook page, and even over phone calls at my office one winter morn-ing in 2012. I was alerted that the media, with their news vans embla-zoned with call letters and radar dishes on the roofs, videographers, and reporters were on their way to the school I was working at the time. The prospect of being accosted by strangers holding microphones seeking to interview me on the spot was terrifying. Public speaking and fifteen minutes of fame have never appealed to me.

The commotion this particular morning involved me as a deaf teacher working in Ann Arbor's public school district—with hearing children! I had been working for well over fifteen years by that time and at first, couldn't figure out why the cause for the sudden ruckus. It turned out to be over a student at Central Michigan University, Kelly Laatsch, profoundly deaf since birth and in her final year of the teacher education program. Ms. Laatsch was in the process of completing her student teaching requirements when she was presented with the Michi-gan Department of Education Teaching Technical Standards, which state that students should "understand and speak in English." The university created an action plan designed to wean Ms. Laatsch off an American Sign Language interpreter, so she could become "independent." If she didn't comply with this plan and pass the technical requirements of stu-dent teaching, she would earn a nonteaching degree or be asked to sign a waiver that said she would not seek a teaching certificate in the state of Michigan.

Understandably, there was statewide furor over her right to accom-modations, including a sign language interpreter, at the university. I would have not minded voicing my concern, but only after I could pull together a statement with poise, grace, and intention, certainly not in a potentially confrontational situation in which I could be placed in a pre-carious spot myself. As it turned out, I never saw the media. My school district did not allow reporters on school grounds, so I was able to for-mulate a statement in the quiet of my home that evening. Fortunately, the kerfuffle quickly blew over when the university backed off and allowed Ms. Laatsch to continue student teaching with accommodations.

It is distressing, after decades of intense advocacy and the enactment of antidiscrimination policies and laws, and even a general climate of political correctness and tolerance, that I *still* hear about deaf and hard of hearing people fighting for their rights to an education that prepares them for employment and for accommodations in the workplace. How-ever, it is heartening that many of these people, including Ms. Laastch, a medical student in Nebraska, a nurse in New York, and others, are actually winning their civil rights suits. Unfortunately, other people also confront an oppressive form of *-isms. Audism, ableism, classism, racism, sexism, heterosexism, nativism, nationalism,* and many other forms of ideologies bring harsh and unfair treatment by one group within a soci-ety to another.

We are now in a national climate of hard conversations about our diversity, limited resources, entitlement, education, and work ethics. Edu-cation policy makers are tackling the vexing issues of achievement gaps, many universities are embracing diversity in their student bodies, and some medical schools are intentionally reaching out to potential medical students from different races, cultures, ethnicities, and (dis)-abilities to represent the diversity of their patient populations. More and more institutions and businesses are aware of antidiscrimination laws and rights to accommodations. Accommodations level the playing field; they are not "handouts." Not only that accommodations are fair, it leads to greater empowerment for the recipient, improved profits for the grantor, and general benefits for the well-being of our society.

Participatory research, in which studies and projects are conducted *with* people and not *on* or *for* people, is receiving more notice in education, public health, and civic engagement. Conversations about equity and privilege are at the forefront, particularly in news media and social networking sites, including headlines and topics, such as Black Lives Matter, immigrants and Dreamers, Islamophobia, nationalism, the 1% in income inequity, and LGBTQ rights. Slowly but surely, people are *listening*. Communities don't become healthy when only a few people are agents of change. *All* of us must be open to linguistic and cultural acceptance. Compassionate listening and positive language that strengthens relationships, collaboration, and empowerment would grace all of us.

NOTES

For personal accounts, I relied on my notes, journals, recollection of events, family stories, and family memorabilia.

PART 1. LANGUAGE
Introduction: Defining Language

Page
3. defining language: Harris, Theodore L., and Richard E. Hodges. *The Literacy Dictionary: The Vocabulary of Reading and Writing*. Newark, NJ: International Reading Association, 1995; Crystal, David. *The Cambridge Encyclopedia of Language*. Vol. 1988. Cambridge, UK: Cambridge University Press, 1987.

Welcome to Dictionopolis!

4. complex, dynamic, and bewildering constellation: Kenneally, Christine. *The First Word: The Search for the Origins of Language*. London: Penguin Books, 2007.

4. *The Phantom Tollbooth*: Juster, Norton. *The Phantom Tollbooth*. New York: Scholastic, 1961.

6. social phenomenon: Stubbs, Michael. "Some Basic Sociolinguistic Concepts," In *The Skin That We Speak: Thoughts on Language and Culture in the Classroom*, ed. Lisa Delpit and Joanne Kilgour Dowdy, 63–85. New York: The New Press, 2002.

6. remaining silent: Kirkland, David E. *A Search Past Silence: The Literacy of Young Black Men*. New York: Teachers College Press, 2013.; Padden, Carol A., and Tom Humphries. *Deaf in America*. Cambridge, MA: Harvard University Press, 1990.

6–7. people with disabilities: Garland-Thomson, Rosemarie. "Becoming Disabled." *The New York Times*, August 19, 2016; Padden, Carol A., and Tom Humphries. *Deaf in America*. Cambridge, MA: Harvard University Press, 1990; Grinspan, Jon. "When Anger Trumped Progress." *The New York Times*, January 16, 2016; Shear, Michael D. and Liam Stack. "Obama Says Movement Like Black Lives Matter 'Can't Just Keep on Yelling.'" *The New York Times*, April 23, 2016; Noddings, Nel, and Laurie Brooks.

Teaching Controversial Issues: The Case for Critical Thinking and Moral Commitment in the Classroom. New York: Teachers College Press, 2016.

Go Figure

11. occupy multiple social groups: Sensoy, Ozlem, and Robin DiAngelo. *Is Everyone Really Equal? An Introduction to Key Concepts in Social Justice Education.* New York: Teachers College Press, 2017.

11. Ruby Bridges: Editors of the Encyclopedia Britannica (The). *Ruby Bridges: American Civil Rights Activist.* Accessed November 16, 2017, https://www.britannica.com/biography/Ruby-Bridges

11. Civil Rights Act: Civil Rights Act of 1964. Public Law 88-352, Title VII, Sec. 703, 78. U.S. Statutes at Large (July 2, 1964).

11. many states continued to exclude: U.S. Office of Special Education Programs. *Twenty-Five Years of Progress in Educating Children with Disabilities through IDEA.* Last modified: 07/19/2007, https://www2.ed.gov/policy/speced/leg/idea/history.html

11. Education for All Handicapped Children Act: Education for All Handicapped Children Act. U.S. Public Law 94-142, U.S. Code. Vol. 20, sec. 1400 et seq. (1975).

14. laws granting protections and access: Americans With Disabilities Act of 1990. Public Law 101-336. 108th Congress, 2nd session (July 26, 1990).

Magic

17. process of learning language: American Speech-Language-Hearing Association. *How Does Your Child Hear and Talk?* Accessed November 16, 2017, http://www.asha.org/public/speech/development/chart/

18. greatest risk to deaf children: Humphries, Tom, Poorna Kushalnagar, Gaurav Mathur, Donna Jo Napoli, Carol Padden, Christian Rathmann, and Scott R. Smith. "Language Acquisition for Deaf Children: Reducing the Harms of Zero Tolerance to the Use of Alternative Approaches." *Harm Reduction Journal* 9, (16). April 2, 2012. Accessed November 16, 2017, http://www.harmreductionjournal.com/content/9/1/16

18. Education for All Handicapped Children Act: Education for All Handicapped Children Act. U.S. Public Law 94-142, U.S. Code. Vol. 20, sec. 1400 et seq. (1975).

19. Head Start: U.S. Department of Health and Human Services, Office of Head Start. *History of Head Start.* Accessed August 13, 2018, https://www.acf.hhs.gov/ohs/about/history-of-head-start

19. Rackham School: Isbell, Egbert R. *A History of Eastern Michigan University: 1849–1965.* Ypsilanti, MI: Eastern Michigan University, 1971. Accessed November 16, 2017, http://commons.emich.edu/books/1/

20. ambiguity of our gestures: Arbib, Michael A. "From Monkey-Like Action Recognition to Human Language: An Evolutionary Framework for Neurolinguistics." *Behavioral and Brain Sciences* 28, no. 2 (2005): 105–124.

20. specific to countries: Simons, Gary F., and Charles D. Fennig, eds. "Languages of the World: Sign Languages." *Ethnologue: Languages of the World, 21st edition.* Dallas, TX, SIL International, 2018. Accessed August 13, 2018, https://www.ethnologue.com/subgroups/sign-language

20. oralism versus manualism: Winefield, Richard. *Never the Twain Shall Meet: Bell, Gallaudet, and the Communications Debate.* Washington, DC: Gallaudet University Press, 1987.

21. not simply sat down and taught: Pinker, S. *The Language Instinct: The New Science of Language and Mind.* London: Penguin Books, 1994.

21. biological timetable: Penfield, Wilder, and Lamar Roberts. *Speech and Brain Mechanisms.* Princeton, NJ: Princeton University Press, 1959.

21. critical period of language acquisition: Lenneberg, Eric H. *Biological Foundations of Language.* New York: John Wiley & Sons, 1967.

21. sensitive (or optimal) period: Werker, Janet F., and Takao K. Hensch. "Critical Periods in Speech Perception: New Directions." *Annual Review of Psychology* 66 (2015), 173–96.

22. topic of a critical period: Crystal, David. *The Cambridge Encyclopedia of Language.* Vol. 1988. Cambridge, UK: Cambridge University Press, 1987.

22. nature and nurture: Coulmas, Florian. *Sociolinguistics: The Study of Speakers' Choices.* New York: Cambridge University Press, 2013.

22. 96 percent have hearing parents: National Association of the Deaf. *Position Statement on Early Cognitive and Language Development and Education of Deaf and Hard of Hearing Children.* June 18, 2014. Accessed November 16, 2017, https://www.nad.org/about-us/position-statements/position-statement-on-early-cognitive-and-language-development-and-education-of-deaf-and-hard-of-hearing-children/

22. babble, they produce all the possible sounds: Kenneally, Christine. *The First Word: The Search for the Origins of Language.* London: Penguin Books, 2007.

22. Children all over the world learn: American Speech-Language-Hearing Association. *Learning Two Languages.* Accessed November 16, 2017, http://www.asha.org/public/speech/development/BilingualChildren/

22–23. advantages to being bilingual: American Speech-Language-Hearing Association. *The Advantages of Being Bilingual.* Accessed November 16, 2017, http://www.asha.org/public/speech/development/The-Advantages-of-Being-Bilingual/

23. National Association of the Deaf: National Association of the Deaf. *Position Statement on ASL and English Bilingual Education.* Accessed September 9, 2018, https://www.nad.org/about-us/position-statements/position-statement-on-asl-and-english-bilingual-education/

PART 2. LISTENING
Introduction: Defining Listening

27. strictly in auditory terms: Merker, Hannah. *Listening: Ways of Hearing in a Silent World.* Dallas: Southern Methodist University Press, 1992.

The Little Terrors

33. Helen Keller: Harrington, Tom. Gallaudet University Library. *FAQ: Deaf People in History/Quotes by Helen Keller.* February 2000. Accessed November 16, 2017, http://libguides.gallaudet.edu/content.php?pid=352126&sid=2881882

33. passive, unquestioned, and superficial: Paul, Richard, and Linda Elder. *Critical Thinking: Learn the Tools the Best Thinkers Use.* Upper Saddle, NJ: Prentice Hall, 2006.

33–34. physiological phenomenon: Barthes, Roland. *The Responsibility of Forms Critical Essays on Music, Art, and Representation.* New York: Hill and Wang, 1985.

34. Listening is the process of: International Listening Association. *Definition of Listening.* 1996. Accessed November 16, 2017, http://www.listen.org

34. Oliver Sacks: Sacks, Oliver. *Seeing Voices: A Journey into the World of the Deaf.* Basingstoke, Hampshire, UK: Pan Macmillan, 2009.

34. I. King Jordan: Gallaudet University. *I. King Jordan.* Accessed November 16, 2017, http://www.gallaudet.edu/about/history-and-traditions/i-king-jordan

One Ball of Confusion

36. Captain Underpants: Pilkey, Dav. *The Adventures of Captain Underpants (Captain Underpants# 1).* New York: Scholastic Inc., 2013.

36. 90- to 120-minute block: Fountas, Irene C., and Gay Su Pinnell. *Guided Reading: Good First Teaching for All Children*. Portsmouth, NH: Heinemann Publishing, 1996.

41. improve acoustics: Acoustical Society of America. *Classroom Acoustics: A Resource for Creating Learning Environments with Desirable Listening Conditions*. May 2003. Accessed November 16, 2017, https://acousticalsociety.org/wp-content/uploads/2018/02/classroom_acoutics_1.pdf

41. Lombard effect: Zollinger, Sue Anne, and Henrik Brumm. "The Lombard Effect." *Current Biology* 21, no. 16 (2011): R614–R615.

41. classroom acoustics: Acoustical Society of America. *Classroom Acoustics: A Resource for Creating Learning Environments with Desirable Listening Conditions*. May 2003. Accessed November 16, 2017, https://acousticalsociety.org/wp-content/uploads/2018/02/classroom_acoutics_1.pdf

42. "the sea of blah": Rowe, Ken. *The Importance of Teaching: Ensuring Better Schooling by Building Teacher Capacities That Maximize the Quality of Teaching and Learning Provision–Implications of Findings from the International and Australian Evidence-Based Research*. Australian Council for Educational Research, 2004. Accessed August 13, 2018, https://research.acer.edu.au/learning_processes/14/

42. speak with brevity: Denton, Paula. *The Power of Our Words: Teacher Language That Helps Children Learn*. Turner Falls, MA: Center for Responsive Schools, Inc., 2013.

42. five dimensions of listening competency: Wolvin, Andrew D., and Steven D. Cohen. "An Inventory of Listening Competency Dimensions." *International Journal of Listening* 26, no. 2 (2012): 64–66.

Second-Grade Otolaryngologist

44. lens of what they *can't do*: Ramsey, Patricia G. *Teaching and Learning in a Diverse World: Multicultural Education for Young Children*. Vol. 93. New York: Teachers College Press, 2004.

46. the ear as a sophisticated organ and causes and types of hearing loss: Johns Hopkins University. *How the Ear Works*. 2015. Accessed August 13, 2018, https://www.hopkinsmedicine.org/healthlibrary/conditions/adult/otolaryngology/how_the_ear_works_22,howtheearworks

48. every act of listening: Haroutunian-Gordon, Sophie. "Listening and Questioning." *Learning Inquiry* 1, no. 2 (2007): 143–52.

Cat and Mouse

50. Uncle Buncle's House: Cowley, Joy. *Uncle Buncle's House.* New York: Wright Group/McGraw-Hill, 1996.

51. narrowly defined and institutionalized view: Smyth, John. "'When Students Have Power': Student Engagement, Student Voice, and the Possibilities for School Reform around 'Dropping Out' of School." *International Journal of Leadership in Education* 9, no. 4 (2006): 285–298.

53. phrase of *good* listening: Bodie, Graham D. "Issues in the Measurement of Listening." *Communication Research Reports* 30, no. 1 (2013): 76–84.

54. eye contact: McDaniel, E. R., L. A. Samovar, and R. E. Porter, eds. "Using Intercultural Communication: The Building Blocks," in *Intercultural Communication: A Reader,* 4–19. Boston: Cengage Learning, 2012.

54. conversational and discourse rules: Carter, Julie A., Janet A. Lees, Gladys M. Murira, Joseph Gona, Brian G. R. Neville, and Charles R. J. C. Newton. "Issues in the Development of Cross-Cultural Assessments of Speech and Language for Children." *International Journal of Language & Communication Disorders* 40, no. 4 (2005): 385–401.

54. met with indifference: Irvine, Jacqueline Jordan. "Complex Relationships between Multicultural Education and Special Education: An African American Perspective." *Journal of Teacher Education* 63, no. 4 (2012): 268–74.

54. teaching that is directive: Haberman, Martin. "The Pedagogy of Poverty Versus Good Teaching." *Phi Delta Kappan* 92, no. 2 (2010): 81–7.

The Help

56. Help can be inadvertently detrimental: Giangreco, Michael F. "One-to-One Paraprofessionals for Students with Disabilities in Inclusive Classrooms: Is Conventional Wisdom Wrong?" *Intellectual and Developmental Disabilities* 48, no. 1 (2010): 1–13.

59. Communication Access Realtime Translation (CART): National Court Reporters Association. *About CART.* Accessed November 16, 2017, https://www.ncra .org/Membership/content.cfm?ItemNumber=9133&navItemNumber=11460

PART 3. SPEAKING
Fonts and Elocution

67. speech and language: American Speech Language Hearing Association. *What Is Speech? What Is Language?* Accessed November 16, 2017, http://www.asha.org/ public/speech/development/language_speech/

69. Good-Night Owl: Hutchins, Pat. *Good-Night, Owl!* New York: Simon and Schuster, 2012.

70. Visemes: Bear, Helen L., and Richard Harvey. "Phoneme-to-Viseme Mappings: The Good, the Bad, and the Ugly." *Speech Communication* 95 (2017): 40–67.

70. physiological phenomenon: Crystal, David. *The Cambridge Encyclopedia of Language.* Vol. 1988. Cambridge, UK: Cambridge University Press, 1987.

Baby Stuff

73. entrenched attitudes and stereotypes: Stubbs, Michael. "Some Basic Sociolinguistic Concepts," In *The Skin That We Speak: Thoughts on Language and Culture in the Classroom*, ed. Lisa Delpit and Joanne Kilgour Dowdy, 63–85. New York: The New Press, 2002.

73. identified as *low-achieving*: Walmsley, Sean A., and Richard L. Allington. "Redefining and Reforming Instructional Support Programs for At-Risk Students." *No Quick Fix: Rethinking Literacy Programs in America's Elementary Schools* 19–44. New York: Teachers College Press, 1995.

75. educated only one in five children with disabilities: U.S. Office of Special Education Programs. "Twenty-Five Years of Progress in Educating Children with Disabilities through IDEA." Last modified: 07/19/2007, https://www2.ed.gov/policy/speced/leg/idea/history.html

75. allowed school districts to refuse: Martin, Edwin W., Reed Martin, and Donna L. Terman. "The Legislative and Litigation History of Special Education," *The Future of Children* 6(1):25-39. 1996): 25–39.

75. incapable of being taught: Mure, G. R. G. *Aristotle*. Oxford: Oxford University Press, 1932. Aristotle. "Posterior Analytics." In *The Works of Aristotle,* ed. W. D. Ross and J. A. Smith, trans. G. R. G. Mure. Oxford: Oxford University Press, 1937.

76. receptive and expressive language: Harris, Theodore L., and Richard E. Hodges. *The Literacy Dictionary: The Vocabulary of Reading and Writing*. Newark, NJ: International Reading Association, 1995.

76. passive knowledge: Stubbs, Michael. "Some Basic Sociolinguistic Concepts," In *The Skin That We Speak: Thoughts on Language and Culture in the Classroom*, ed. Lisa Delpit and Joanne Kilgour Dowdy, 63–85. New York: The New Press, 2002.

76. more pronounced for bilingual speakers: Keller, Karin, Larissa M. Troesch, and Alexander Grob. "A Large Receptive–Expressive Gap in Bilingual Children." *Frontiers in Psychology* 6 (2015): 1284 *PMC*. Web. 9 Sept. 2018.

76. ontological positions and recognizing children's agency: Gallagher, Michael. (2008). "Data Collection and Analysis" in *Researching with Children and Young People: Research Design, Methods and Analysis* ed. Kay Tisdall, John M. Davis, and Michael Gallagher. Thousand Oaks, CA: Sage, 2008.

77. Rights of the Child: United Nations "Convention on the Rights of the Child." *Child Labor* (1989): 8.

PART 4. CONVERSATION
Two Truths and a Lie

82. hearing children in families with deaf or hard of hearing parents: Singleton, Jenny L., and Matthew D. Tittle. *A Guide for Professionals Serving Hearing Children with Deaf Parents.* Champaign, IL: University of Illinois at Urbana-Champaign, 2001.; Wolter, Deborah L. and Kathleen Quinn. "Young Children in Families with a Parent with Hearing Loss." *Hearing Loss* 20, no. 4 (1999), 16–18.

86. 2008 Super Bowl commercial: Bob's House - Pepsi Super Bowl Ad. https://www.youtube.com/watch?v=ffrq6cUoE5A

Skipping Stones

88. taught in a disabling context: Wolter, Deborah L. *Reading Upside Down: Identifying and Addressing Opportunity Gaps in Literacy Instruction.* New York: Teachers College Press, 2015.

88. feature of the Russian sound system: Smith, Bernard. *Learner English: A Teacher's Guide to Interference and Other Problems.* Stuttgart, Germany: Ernst Klett Sprachen, 2001.

Eyes in the Back of My Head

96. pragmatic language: American Speech-Language-Hearing Association. *Social Communication.* Accessed November 16, 2017, http://www.asha.org/public/speech/development/Pragmatics/

96. invisible disability: Tada, Joni Eareckson. *How Do You Define Invisible Disability?* Invisible Disabilities Association. Accessed November 16, 2017, https://invisibledisabilities.org/what-is-an-invisible-disability/

99. no need to adhere to rigidity: McDaniel, E. R., L. A. Samovar, and R. E. Porter, eds. "Using Intercultural Communication: The Building Blocks," in *Intercultural Communication: A Reader,* 4–19. Boston: Cengage Learning, 2012.

Part 5. Reading
Introduction: Defining Reading

103. Reading defined: Harris, Theodore L., and Richard E. Hodges. *The Literacy Dictionary: The Vocabulary of Reading and Writing*. Newark, NJ: International Reading Association, 1995.

103. belief that reading requires the ability to decode: National Association of the Deaf. *Position Statement on Early Cognitive and Language Development and Education of Deaf and Hard of Hearing Children*. June 18, 2014. Accessed November 16, 2017, https://www.nad.org/about-us/position-statements/position-statement-on-early-cognitive-and-language-development-and-education-of-deaf-and-hard-of-hearing-children/

The Poetry Slam

107. particularly boys of color: Kirkland, David E. *A Search Past Silence: The Literacy of Young Black Men*. New York: Teachers College Press, 2013.

110. Civil Rights Act of 1964: Civil Rights Act of 1964. Public Law 88-352, Title VII, Sec. 703, 78. U.S. Statutes at Large (July 2, 1964).

110. Education for All Handicapped Children Act of 1975: Education for All Handicapped Children Act. U.S. Public Law 94-142, U.S. Code. Vol. 20, sec. 1400 et seq. (1975).

110. within-school segregation: Tyson, Karolyn. "Tracking Segregation, and the Opportunity Gap," in *Closing the Opportunity Gap: What America Must Do To Give Every Child an Even Chance*, ed. Prudence L. Carter and Kevin G. Welner 169–180. New York: Oxford University Press, 2013.

110. literacy and education are by far not interchangeable: Taylor, Denny, and Catherine Dorsey-Gaines. *Growing Up Literate: Learning from Inner-City Families*. Portsmouth, NH: Heinemann Educational Books, Inc., 1988.

110. many kinds of literacy: Harris, Theodore L., and Richard E. Hodges. *The Literacy Dictionary: The Vocabulary of Reading and Writing*. Newark, NJ: International Reading Association, 1995.

111. number of cultures coexist: Ferdman, Bernardo. "Literacy and Cultural Identity." *Harvard Educational Review* 60, no. 2 (1990): 181–205.

111. use the term *literacies*: Lazar, Althier M., Patricia Ann Edwards, and Gwendolyn Thompson McMillon. *Bridging Literacy and Equity: The Essential Guide to Social Equity Teaching*. New York: Teachers College Press, 2012.

111. similar to that of the test makers: Loewen, James W. *Lies My Teacher Told Me: Everything Your American History Textbook Got Wrong.* New York: The New Press, 2008.

Oh, Gee

113. readers use multiple strategies: Clay, Marie M. *An Observation Survey of Early Literacy Achievement.* Portsmouth, NH: Heinmann Educational Books, Inc., 2013.; Routman, Regie. *Transitions: From Literature to Literacy.* Portsmouth, NH: Heinemann Educational Books, Inc., 1988.

115. metalinguistic awareness: Harris, Theodore L., and Richard E. Hodges. *The Literacy Dictionary: The Vocabulary of Reading and Writing.* Newark, NJ: International Reading Association, 1995.

115. dyslexia definition: U.S. Department of Education. "Topic: Identification of Specific Learning Disabilities." Accessed November 16, 2017, http://www.ldonline.org/article/11202/

115. lack of quality literacy: International Literacy Association. "Dyslexia (Research Advisory)." Newark, DE: Author, 2016.

115. justifiable to consider phonemic awareness: Johnson, D. "Dyslexia," in *The Literacy Dictionary*, ed. T. Harris, & R. E. Hodges, 64. Newark, DE: International Reading Association, 1995.

116. Orton-Gillingham approach: Academy of Orton-Gillingham Practitioners and Educators. *Home Page.* Accessed November 16, 2017, http://www.ortonacademy.org/

116. controversial with inconsistent research results: International Literacy Association. *Home Page.* Accessed November 16, 2017, https://www.literacyworldwide.org/; Johns Hopkins University School of Education Center for Data-Driven Reform in Education. "Best Evidence Encyclopedia." Accessed November 16, 2017, http://www.bestevidence.org/; Institute of Education Services, National Center for Education Evaluation and Regional Assistance. *What Works Clearinghouse.* Accessed August 13, 2018, https://ies.ed.gov/ncee/wwc/

117. targeted outcomes are identical: Gibson, Sharan A., and Barbara Moss. *Every Young Child a Reader: Using Marie Clay's Key Concepts for Classroom Instruction.* New York: Teachers College Press, 2016.

Dribbling Vowels

119. Aoccdrnig to rscheearch at Cmabrigde uinervtisy: Internet meme.

122. Accents and syntaxes: Birner, Betty. "Why Do Some People Have an Accent?" Brochure from the Linguistic Society of America, 1999. Retrieved from www.linguisticsociety.org/content/why-do-some-people-have-accent

A Village

127. Television shows of the 1970s: *The Flintstones, The Jetsons, The Bugs Bunny Show, The Rocky and Bullwinkle Show, Scooby Doo, Yogi Bear, Gilligan's Island, The Munsters, Star Trek Flipper, Mr. Ed,* and *Lassie.*

127. Children's books mentioned: *Hop on Pop* (Dr. Seuss); *Put Me in the Zoo* (Robert Lopshire); *The Whingdingdilly* (Bill Peet); *Huge Harold* (Bill Peet); *The Little House* (Virginia Lee Burton); *Too Much Noise* (Ann McGovern); *Where the Wild Things Are* (Maurice Sendak); *The Snowy Day* (Ezra Jack Keats); *Mr. Gumpy's Outing* (John Burningham); *Clifford, the Big Red Dog* (Norman Bridwell); *Frog and Toad Together* (Arnold Lobel).

PART 6. WRITING

Finger Painting

140. most cognitively demanding tasks: Farrall, Melissa Lee. *Reading Assessment: Linking Language, Literacy, and Cognition.* Hoboken, NJ: John Wiley & Sons, 2012.

Jiraf, Tutul, and Bune

143. *Mr. Gumpy's Outing:* Birmingham, John. *Mr. Gumpy's Outing.* Square Fish, a subsidiary of U.S. Macmillan, 1990.

146. historical and linguistic roots: Crystal, David. *The Cambridge Encyclopedia of Language.* Vol. 1988. Cambridge, UK: Cambridge University Press, 1987.

146. inconsistencies and exceptions: Linan-Thompson, Sylvia, and Sharon Vaughn. *Research-based Methods of Reading Instruction for English Language Learners, Grades K-4.* Alexandria, VA: Association for Supervision and Curriculum Development, 2007.

146. spelling reform: Halladay, T. *Heroes of Spelling Reform.* English Spelling Society, 2008. Accessed November 16, 2017, http://spellingsociety.org/uploaded_leaflets/2008heroes-leaflet.pdf

"'Nother Stinkin' 'Signment"

148. notable or influential women of color: Sally Hemings: *Thomas Jefferson Foundation. The life of Sally Hemings. Accessed September 9, 2018,* https://www.monticello.org/sallyhemings/; **Henrietta Lacks:** Skloot, Rebecca. *The Immortal Life of Henrietta Lacks.* New York: Crown Publishers, 2010; **Ruby Bridges:** *National Women's History Museum. Ruby Bridges. Accessed September 9, 2018,* https://www.womenshistory.org/education-resources/biographies/ruby-bridges; **Shirley Chisholm:** *National Women's History Museum. Shirley Chisholm. Accessed September 9, 2018,*

https://www.womenshistory.org/education-resources/biographies/shirley-chisholm;
Human computers: Shetterly, Margot Lee. *Hidden Figures: The American Dream and the Untold Story of the Black Women Mathematicians Who Helped Win the Space Race.* First edition. New York: William Morrow, 2016.

151. few languages have ever been written down: Crystal, David. *The Cambridge Encyclopedia of Language.* Vol. 1988. Cambridge, UK: Cambridge University Press, 1987.

151. 6,000 years old: Kenneally, Christine. *The First Word: The Search for the Origins of Language.* London: Penguin Books, 2007.

151. formal features of writing: Crystal, David. *The Cambridge Encyclopedia of Language.* Vol. 1988. Cambridge, UK: Cambridge University Press, 1987.

151. intonation and gesture: Kenneally, Christine. *The First Word: The Search for the Origins of Language.* London: Penguin Books, 2007.

151. phonemic awareness: Harris, Theodore L., and Richard E. Hodges. *The Literacy Dictionary: The Vocabulary of Reading and Writing.* Newark, NJ: International Reading Association, 1995.

Marginalia

153. livestream of April, the giraffe: Animal Adventures Park (The). *April the Giraffe Page.* Accessed September 19, 2018, https://aprilthegiraffe.com/

154. personal marks in the margins of books: O'Connell, Mark. "The Marginal Obsession with Marginalia." *The New Yorker,* January 26, 2012. Accessed November 16, 2017, http://www.newyorker.com/books/page-turner/the-marginal-obsession-with-marginalia

PART 7. LITERACIES
Introduction: Defining Literacies

161. definition of *literacy* is complex, controversial, and dynamic: Ferdman, Bernardo. "Literacy and Cultural Identity." *Harvard Educational Review* 60, no. 2 (1990): 181–205; Venezky, Richard L., Daniel A Wagner, and Barrie S. Ciliberti. *Toward Defining Literacy.* Newark, DE: International Literacy Association, 1990; Taylor, Denny, and Catherine Dorsey-Gaines. *Growing Up Literate: Learning from Inner-City Families.* Portsmouth, NH: Heinemann, 1988; Lazar, Althier M., Patricia Ann Edwards, and Gwendolyn Thompson McMillon. *Bridging Literacy and Equity: The Essential Guide to Social Equity Teaching.* New York: Teachers College Press, 2012.

Nosy

164. Children's books mentioned: *Misty of Chincoteague* (Marguerite Henry); *Stuart Little* (E. B. White); *Charlotte's Web* (E. B. White); *Little House in the Big Woods* (Ingalls Wilder); *Little House on the Prairie* (Ingalls Wilder); *Charlie and the Chocolate Factory* (Roald Dahl); *James and the Giant Peach* (Roald Dahl); *Wind in the Willows* (Kenneth Grahame).

166. Comic books mentioned: *Richie Rich* (Alfred Harvey and Warren Kremer); *Peanuts* (Charles Schulz); *Archie Comics* (John L. Goldwater and Bob Montana).

The Gargoyles

169. 171,476 words in current use: Oxford University Press. *How Many Words Are There in the English Language?* Accessed November 16, 2017, https://en.oxforddictionaries.com/explore/how-many-words-are-there-in-the-english-language

169. acquiring vocabulary appropriate: Hermans, Daan, Loes Wauters, Margot Willemsen, and Harry Knoors. "Vocabulary Acquisition in Deaf and Hard-of-Hearing Children," in *The Oxford Handbook of Deaf Studies in Language*, ed. Marc Marschark and Patricia Elizabeth Spencer. New York: Oxford University Press, 2003.

171. literacy as owned by the schools: Kirkland, David E. *A Search Past Silence: The Literacy of Young Black Men.* New York: Teachers College Press, 2013.

171. linguistic structures: Werker, Janet F., and Takao K. Hensch. "Critical Periods in Speech Perception: New Directions." *Annual Review of Psychology* 66 (2015).

171. linguistic input that children receive Hermans, Daan, Loes Wauters, Margot Willemsen, and Harry Knoors. "Vocabulary Acquisition in Deaf and Hard-of-Hearing Children," in *The Oxford Handbook of Deaf Studies in Language*, ed. Marc Marschark and Patricia Elizabeth Spencer. New York: Oxford University Press, 2015; Hart, Betty, and Todd R. Risley. "The Early Catastrophe: The 30 Million Word Gap by Age 3." *American Educator* 27, no. 1 (2003): 4–9.

172. linguistic overprotection: Calderon, Rosemary, and Mark Greenberg. "Social and Emotional Development of Deaf Children." *Oxford Handbook of Deaf Studies, Language, and Education* 1 (2003): 177.

Snap, Crackle, Pop

175. our nation's fourth-graders: National Assessment of Education Progress. *The Nation's Report Card 2016. How Did U.S. Students Perform on the Most Recent Assessments?* https://www.nationsreportcard.gov/

175. certain letters and sounds pair up: Bill, Bryson. *Mother Tongue: English and How it Got That Way.* London: Penguin Books, 1990.

176. literacy tests: Hartford, Bruce. *Voting Rights: Are You 'Qualified' To Vote? Take a 'Literacy Test' To Find Out. Literacy Tests and Voter Applications.* Civil Rights Movement Veterans. Accessed November 16, 2017, http://www.crmvet.org/info/lithome.htm

The Odyssey

180. dedicated search for meaning: Noddings, Nel, and Laurie Brooks. *Teaching Controversial Issues: The Case for Critical Thinking and Moral Commitment in the Classroom.* New York: Teachers College Press, 2016.

182. High school books mentioned: *The Great Gatsby* (F. Scott Fitzgerald); *Grapes of Wrath* (John Steinbeck); *Macbeth* (William Shakespeare); *Fahrenheit 451* (Ray Bradbury); *The Old Man and the Sea* (Ernest Hemingway); *A Tale of Two Cities* (Charles Dickens); *One Flew Over the Cuckoo's Nest* (Ken Kesey); *Uncle Tom's Cabin* (Harriet Beecher Stowe); *The Odyssey* (Homer).

184. conform to safe and neutral ideas: Noddings, Nel, and Laurie Brooks. *Teaching Controversial Issues: The Case for Critical Thinking and Moral Commitment in the Classroom.* New York: Teachers College Press, 2016.

184. participatory democracy: Noddings, Nel, and Laurie Brooks. *Teaching Controversial Issues: The Case for Critical Thinking and Moral Commitment in the Classroom.* New York: Teachers College Press, 2016.

185. literacy and education not interchangeable: Taylor, Denny, and Catherine Dorsey-Gaines. *Growing Up Literate: Learning from Inner-City Families.* Portsmouth, NH: Heinemann, 1988.

185. richness of their heritages and experiences: Morrow, Lesley Mandel, Jeanne Paratore, Devron Gaber, Colin Harrison, and Diane Tracey. "Family Literacy: Perspective and Practices." *The Reading Teacher* 47, no. 3 (1993): 194–200.

PART 8. LINGUISTICS

Introduction: Defining Linguistics

189. Defining linguistics and sociolinguistics: Labov, William. "Objectivity and Commitment in Linguistic Science: The Case of the Black English Trial in Ann Arbor." *Language in Society* 11, no. 2 (1982): 165–201; Bucholtz, Mary, Audrey Lopez, Allina Mojarro, Elena Skapoulli, Chris VanderStouwe, and Shawn Warner-Garcia. "Sociolinguistic Justice in the Schools: Student Researchers as Linguistic Experts." *Language and Linguistics Compass* 8, no. 4 (2014): 144–57.

Speak English

195. manifestly unfair: Stubbs, Michael. "Some Basic Sociolinguistic Concepts," In *The Skin That We Speak: Thoughts on Language and Culture in the Classroom*, ed. Lisa Delpit and Joanne Kilgour Dowdy, 63–85. New York: The New Press, 2002.

195. older one gets, the harder: Birner, Betty. "Why Do Some People Have an Accent?" Brochure from the Linguistic Society of America, 1999. Retrieved from www.linguisticsociety.org/content/why-do-some-people-have-accent

195. communicate effectively: American Speech-Language-Hearing Association. *Communication for a Lifetime.* Accessed November 16, 2017, http://www.asha.org/public/

195. language gets the job done: Everett, Daniel. *How Language Began: The Story of Humanity's Greatest Invention.* London, Profile Books, 2017.

195. reality is that *all* speakers: American Association for Applied Linguistics. *Position Paper on Accents: AAAL Resolution against Discrimination on the Basis of Accented Speech (February 2011).* Accessed November 16, 2017, http://www.aaal .org/?page=PositionStatements&hhSearchTerms=%22accents%22#Feb%202011

The Ann Arbor Decision

198. *Ann Arbor Decision:* Martin Luther King Jr., etc., v. Ann Arbor Sch. Dist., 473 F. Supp. 1371 - Dist Court, ED Michigan 1979 (The Ann Arbor Decision).Accessed August 13, 2018, https://scholar.google.com/scholar_case?q=Martin+Luther+King+Junior+Elementary+School+Children+et+al.+v.+Ann+Arbor+-School+District&hl=en&as_sdt=2003&case=2263977517061661993&scilh=0

200. when we identify one thing as like the others: Minow, Martha. *Making All the Difference: Inclusion, Exclusion, and American Law.* Ithaca, NY: Cornell University Press, 1990.

201. Inclusion can be compatible: Florian, Lani, Kristine Black-Hawkins, and Martyn Rouse. *Achievement and Inclusion in Schools.* Abingdon, UK: Routledge, 2016.

PART 9. CONCLUSION
Kerfuffles and Knickers in a Knot!

207. The bystander effect: Eyes on Bullying. Education Development Center. *What Can You Do? Bystander.* Accessed September 9, 2018, http://www.eyesonbullying.org/bystander.html

207. Kelly Laatsch: Central Michigan Life. *Deaf Student May Not Graduate with Teaching Degree Because of Interpreter Regulations. Central Michigan Life*, February 23, 2012. Accessed November 16, 2017, http://www.cm-life.com/article/2012/02/deaf-student-may-not-graduate-because-of-regulations#disqus_thread

208. medical student in Nebraska: National Association of the Deaf. "Deaf Medical Student Wins ADA Against Creighton." September 5, 2013. Accessed November 16, 2017, https://www.nad.org/2013/09/05/deaf-medical-student-wins-ada-case-against -creighton/

208. nurse in New York: Association of Medical Professionals with Hearing Losses. *Breaking: Deaf Nurse Wins Court Case.* January 21, 2016. Accessed November 16, 2017, https://amphl.org/breaking-deaf-nurse-wins-court-case/